The Diplomatic Retreat *of* France
and Public Opinion *on the* Eve *of*
the French Revolution, *1783–1789*

ORVILLE T. MURPHY

The Diplomatic Retreat *of*

France *and* Public Opinion

on the Eve *of the*

French Revolution, *1783–1789*

The Catholic University of America Press

WASHINGTON, D.C.

Library of Congress Cataloguing-in-Publication Data
Murphy, Orville Theodore.
The diplomatic retreat of France and public opinion on
the eve of the French Revolution, 1783–1789 / Orville T.
Murphy.
  p.   cm.
Includes bibliographical references and index.
  1. France—History—Revolution, 1789–1799—Causes.
2. France—Foreign relations—Europe.   3. Europe—
Foreign relations—France.   4. France—Foreign public
opinion.   5. Diplomacy—Public opinion.   I. Title.
  DC138.M85   1997
  327.44'009'033—dc21
  96-53231
  ISBN 0-8132-0892-0

Contents

PART III. Public Opinion

Acknowledgments

No historian completes a book without a profound sense of gratitude to all those persons who contributed directly or indirectly to his scholarship. Charles Daniello and the librarians at Lockwood Library at the State University of New York at Buffalo supported my research for many decades through lush times and budget cuts, through creative periods and fallow slumps. To them I owe a special thank you.

The archivists at the Archives des Affaires Étrangères at the Quai d'Orsay in Paris, France, once again provided me for extended periods of time with courteous and extraordinarily competent support. At the Archives Diplomatiques de Nantes, Monsieur Pascal Even and staff labored beyond the call of duty to ensure that when I left Nantes I had seen and photocopied *all* the documents needed to complete my research.

I am grateful to the staff of the British Museum for permission to use two cartoons by the Hanoverian artist Johann Heinrich Ramberg, depicting France's diplomatic humiliation in the Dutch crisis of 1787 (Chapter 6). I owe thanks to Professor Marie Donaghay for sending me the cartoons.

The close and critical reading of my manuscript by Professors Marsha L. Frey and Thomas J. Schaeper rescued me from the embarrassment of several errors and provided me with numerous suggestions for improvement. The alert attention of those at The

Catholic University of America Press has been supportive and helpful. Thanks to director, David McGonagle, to editor, Susan Needham, and to marketing manager, Elizabeth A. Benevides. While I am responsible for any residual errors, fumbles, or gross violations of the *Chicago Manual of Style*, the above persons are responsible for the fact that there are fewer now than before the manuscript fell into their capable hands.

Most of all, thanks to my wife, Carolyn, and my family. Their love and gentle tolerance of an historian in their midst flavors all my projects with joy. This book is dedicated to Devin and Harrison, my grandsons, and to Hannah, my granddaughter.

ORVILLE T. MURPHY
Kirkland, Washington

The Diplomatic Retreat *of* France *and* Public Opinion *on the* Eve *of the* French Revolution, *1783–1789*

Introduction

"Much has been said about the causes of the [French] Revolution. . . . One of the most important, in my opinion, is the change in the international position of France which brought the government into deep discredit."

LEOPOLD VON RANKE (1833)

THIS BOOK is about the collapse of French power in the European system of great powers on the eve of the French Revolution. It is also about the French public's opinion of that decline and the causes of the French Revolution.

The settlement of the War of the American Revolution in 1783 provided French statesmen with the brilliant illusion that, once again, the French monarch sat as arbiter of Europe. It took only six short years to destroy that illusion. By late 1788, the comte de Montmorin, Louis XVI's secretary of state for foreign affairs, complained that he was overwhelmed. Harassed with diplomatic humiliations abroad and a financial crisis at home, he busied himself with a memoir concerned with how his office was to cope with huge cuts in the ordinary budget of his department.[1] He felt

---

1. "Project des fonds à régler pour le service des Affaires Etrangères pendant l'année 1789," Archives Diplomatique, Nantes, Series: Comptabilité, carton 63.

trapped, he said, in "the rigor of circumstances." In 1790 some of Louis XVI's diplomatic representatives who served in foreign courts began to resign their posts. Or they simply, unofficially, walked away and left their embassies in the care of their secretaries. They had taken an oath to the king of France, they said. They were not ambassadors or ministers of the French "nation" or that strange new entity, the "people of France."[2] All this in sharp contrast to the joy and deep satisfaction that had accompanied the peace of 1783. The victory of 1783 was only a "brilliant interlude" on the secular curve of long-term decline.[3]

While this study is concerned with the few critical years between the end of the American Revolutionary War and the beginning of the French Revolution, France's "effacement" as a great power began long before resignations of diplomats signaled the disintegration of France's diplomatic corps.[4] France's distresses originated, in part, during the latter years of the reign of Louis XIV,[5] they multiplied with increasing force with the exhausting War of Austrian Succession (1740–48), and spread onto a worldwide stage after the ill-fated reversal of alliances of 1756, known as the "Diplomatic Revolution," produced new great-power alignments and the Seven Years' War (1756–63). France's troubles grew also from the

2. Louis Bergès, "Le Roi ou la nation? Un débat de conscience après Varennes entre diplomates français (juillet 1791)," *Revue d'histoire diplomatique*, nos. 1–2 (1984), 31–46.

3. Albert Sorel, *L'Europe et la Révolution Française* (Paris, 1885), 1:300–302.

4. I have borrowed the term "effacement" from Jean-Jules Clamageran, *Histoire de l'impôt en France, depuis l'époque romaine jusqu'a 1774* (Geneva: Slatkine Reprints, 1980), 3:384. Clamageran used it to condemn the policies of the Duc d'Aiguillon: "Ce n'est plus une politique de paix, c'est une politique d'effacement." I use the term (without the harsh judgmental overtones intended by Clamageran) to mean "to erase, to make disappear, to withdraw."

5. Albert Sorel, *L'Europe et la Révolution Française* (Paris, 1885), 1:195; A recent study by Bailey Stone does an excellent job tracing the long-term erosion of France's military/diplomatic position. *The Genesis of the French Revolution: A Global-Historical Interpretation.* (Cambridge, 1994).

relative rise and decline of the military might and influence of several major European powers, from rearmament and war in the Baltic, from instability and war in Eastern Europe, and from a new English-Prussian understanding, which brought Britain out of the isolation of the American Revolutionary War and reintroduced British influence on the Continent with an alarming effectiveness. The crushing of the pro-French Patriots in the Dutch Republic by the Prussian army in 1787 was a dramatic confirmation of the French retreat, but the ambiguities and setbacks of France's policies in Eastern Europe were much more destructive of France's long-term influence in Europe. British and Prussian assistance to Gustavus III of Sweden in the Russo-Swedish war of 1788 all but replaced France's influence in Sweden and the Baltic and left France's ambassador in Stockholm with little to do there but passively observe France's enemies prop up France's staggering ally.

Despite his efforts to change France's relation with Britain, Louis XVI never achieved a détente with London. On several occasions when his allies made decisions ruinous to French interests, Louis XVI was not even consulted. When decisive international conflicts reached the flash point of war, Louis XVI could not provide his allies with expected military and diplomatic support. He had decided, quite wisely in retrospect, that France's finances and domestic problems did not permit military adventures and that peace was essential to France's regeneration. Faced with these changes, France's statesmen and diplomats were often frustrated. As their influence declined, they were confronted with discontented allies and they were ignored or pushed aside. Consequently, they failed to achieve what they had committed themselves to accomplish. In a domestic political climate where public opinion played a critical role, these changes brought discredit to the government and to the monarchy.

What happens to a society in the habit of playing a major role among the great powers when circumstances and scarce resources force a retreat? In the case of France on the eve of the French Revolution, the response was humiliation, anger, and disaffection, all of which quickly became politicized. Aristocratic military officers whose very identities were defined by wars and preparations for war, could see nothing but cowardice and dishonor in the retreat from international competition. In the government, those who read the discouraging numbers generated by the royal treasury could see no alternative but France's retreat, although they hoped it would be only temporary. By 1786 the costs of servicing the loans floated to pay for wars and foreign policy were running nearly one-half of the annual ordinary budget. Borrowing to pay for wars, diplomatic relations, and gifts and subsidies to friends and allies was not unusual. By the end of the eighteenth century, every great power in Europe did it. But the British Parliament always raised taxes to pay for war loans. The despotic Russian rulers did the same, but with more brutality. Despite their claims to the title of absolute monarch, Louis XV and Louis XVI always found themselves at the center of a political firestorm whenever they tried to raise taxes to pay for their loans. Consequently, to appease public opinion they postponed the inevitable day when the costs of interests, charges, and promises came due. In 1786 that day arrived.

Meanwhile, the French Parlement repeatedly and successfully obstructed Louis XVI's plans for tax reform while simultaneously gaining the support of the public in doing so. Scandals in the Paris stock exchange further eroded trust in the integrity of government officials. The bitter and public debate about Louis's 1786 commercial treaty with Britain fostered the false but nevertheless damaging notion that, in signing the treaty, Louis had recklessly compromised the French economy. The failure of the government and the Assemblies of Notables in 1787 and 1788 to find a solution to France's accumulating financial problems provided further evidence for the opinion that France's monarchy was no longer up to the task of governing France.

Thus, diplomatic troubles accompanied the pre-revolutionary

domestic crisis that settled over France after 1786. These troubles eroded confidence in the authority and capabilities of the French crown, a confidence already severely weakened by the domestic crisis. The public perceived (mistakenly) that its monarchy was either out of touch with foreign affairs or that it cared nothing for the fundamental interests or prestige of France. Furthermore, public opinion perceived (correctly) that the respect and authority France usually enjoyed in Europe's diplomatic affairs had all but disappeared in a hammering series of diplomatic retreats. The king, it appeared, was either indifferent or ineffective or, at best, surrounded by incompetent, corrupt, or cowardly ministers. These ideas insinuated themselves into every discussion of domestic policy, of financial reform, and of foreign affairs. In this way, foreign affairs played an active role in the coming of the French Revolution.

The relation between French foreign affairs and the French Revolution receives only partial and uneven attention in the conventional studies of the origins of the French Revolution. In his classic *The Coming of the French Revolution*, Georges Lefebvre devotes a paragraph to the idea that the pre-revolutionary crisis goes back to the costs of the American Revolutionary War, another paragraph to the effect on public opinion of the Anglo-French Commercial Treaty of 1786, and a sentence on the economic impact in France of the Russo-Turkish War of 1787.[6] The *Longman Companion to the French Revolution* devotes two sentences to issues of foreign affairs in its section on the "Pre-revolution," and says almost nothing about how foreign affairs might have been an element in the pre-revolutionary ferment.[7] J. F. Bosher rectifies the

6. Georges Lefebvre, *The Coming of the French Revolution* (Princeton, 1947), 21, 104–5.

7. Colin Jones, *The Longman Companion to the French Revolution* (New York, 1988), 4–5. The two sentences mention the Anglo-French Commercial Treaty (1786) and the domestic crisis of the Dutch Republic (1787). While his later discussion of the Anglo-French Commercial Treaty (pp. 9 and 302) suggests that there may have been a relation between the treaty and popular revolt, the section "International Relations and War" deals only with diplomacy and foreign affairs *after* 1789.

imbalance somewhat with more than two pages of discussion of foreign policy and the coming of the Revolution. He quotes Albert Sorel to the effect that on the eve of the Revolution "Public Opinion in France unanimously desired the restoration of French prestige abroad."[8] Sorel was probably one of the few historians who understood the relation between foreign affairs, French public opinion, and the coming of the French Revolution.[9]

In his study of the French Revolution, Simon Schama clearly recognizes the relation between the American Revolutionary War, the French failures in the Dutch crisis, and the subversive effects of these events on the authority of the French monarchy and the health of French finances. But France's foreign relations on the eve of the Revolution were not limited to the Dutch and American republics. In his study of the "desacralization" of the French monarchy, Jeffrey Merrick does not include the role of foreign affairs in the process he describes.[10] In his excellent biography of Louis XVI, John Hardman devotes an entire chapter to Louis's foreign policy. But Hardman leaves unexplored the relation between the public perceptions of foreign affairs and the outbreak of the Revolution.[11] Bailey Stone's recent *The Genesis of the French Revolution: A Global-Historical Interpretation* deals with the seventeenth- and eighteenth-century diplomatic and domestic background to the French Revolution. Stone provides the long-term view that is the context for this study. He also recognizes the relation between France's weakening diplomatic position and negative public opinion. Thus, in many important ways, Stone's sholarship complements my own.[12]

8. J. F. Bosher, *The French Revolution* (New York, 1988), 76–78.

9. See, especially, Albert Sorel, *L'Europe et la Révolution Française* (Paris, 1885), 1:296–310.

10. Simon Schama, *Citizens: A Chronicle of the French Revolution* (New York, 1989), 21–49; 60–71; 248–53. Jeffrey W. Merrick, *The Descralization of the French Monarchy in the Eighteenth Century* (Baton Rouge, La., 1990).

11. John Hardman, *Louis XVI* (New Haven, 1993).

12. Bailey Stone, *The Genesis of the French Revolution*, 58–63, 80–81, and passim.

Whereas his focus is on British foreign policy, Jeremy Black's *British Foreign Policy in an Age of Revolution; 1783–1793* provides a helpful model in his treatment of the interaction between foreign policy and domestic politics.[13]

. The assumptions of this book fit easily within the broad framework of Paul Kennedy's *The Rise and Fall of the Great Powers.*[14] Kennedy argues that the ability of a state to sustain the burden of great-power status is directly related to the availability and effective use of its economic and financial resources. Over the long run, when a state overextends itself in foreign affairs beyond its "productive and revenue raising capacities" it runs the risks of falling into a decline relative to the other states in the international system. In his discussion of France from 1787 to the Revolution, Kennedy rightly argues that France's inability to play a more decisive role in European diplomatic affairs was directly related to Louis XVI's inability to tap the enormous wealth of France to finance an energetic foreign policy.[15]

But while Kennedy clearly defines the relation between France's internal crises and its decline in the international arena, he fails to see how foreign affairs in turn influenced the domestic and political crises themselves. Just as an adequate theory of war must allow for the mutual interaction of domestic and foreign forces, so must an adequate theory of international relations.[16] Kennedy's treatment of the movements of states in and out of the category of "great power" following exhaustive wars and preparations for war is persuasive, but his broad sketches often suggest that history endlessly repeats itself. Sweden in the seventeenth century, France late in the eighteenth century, Russia in the nineteenth century, and

13. Jeremy Black, *British Foreign Policy in an Age of Revolution: 1783–1793* (Cambridge, 1994).

14. Paul Kennedy, *The Rise and Fall of the Great Powers* (New York, 1987).

15. Ibid., 121.

16. T. C. W. Blanning, *The Origins of the French Revolutionary Wars* (London and New York, 1986), 19–29.

Great Britain in the twentieth century all went into decline after having enjoyed the status of great powers. Humans, too, are born, flourish, and then decline, but *how* they do this is what distinguishes one person's history from another and separates mechanical formulae from tragedy and farce.

Why France (or any other nation) chose to war so frequently in the eighteenth century is an enigma provoking endless debate. Some psychologists see the innate aggressiveness of human beings as biologically built into the human psyche—the result, perhaps, of the long evolutionary struggle for survival. When the aggressive instincts collide or confront another instinct, such as that of territoriality, war is the result. But a significant number of anthropologists disagree with the thesis of innate aggression. Human aggression, they claim, is not innate but is derived from a real or perceived interference in a basic biological function, such as sex or hunger, or from the frustration of some culturally created purpose, such as ownership or ideology. Also, as T. C. W. Blanning points out in his excellent summary of these theories, none of them can explain why the same nations who fight wars sometimes choose peace.[17] More to the point, such theories fail to provide any help at all when we ask why France went to war so many times in the eighteenth century and then did not to go to war in the Dutch crisis of 1786–87.

Historians usually prefer less abstract explanations of how nations behave. Geoffrey Blainey, in his study of war, offers a set of observations which, when modified to fit the particular case, are especially relevant to understanding France's military and diplomatic role in the eighteenth century.[18] Following Blainey, I have assumed that war and peace, as well as other diplomatic activities of France, followed from the decisions of individuals. The decisions, in turn, were based on estimates of France's own military strength and diplomatic influence and whether or not those

17. Ibid., 1–35.
18. Geoffrey Blainey, *The Causes of War* (Melbourne, 1977).

strengths could be used in the anticipated theatres of concern. Considerations of the military strength and diplomatic influence of other nations and how they might behave should a diplomatic crisis or war occur also informed decisions. In addition, foreign policy decisions were decided on the basis of assessments about internal unity in France and in the lands of allies and enemies. Decisions also flowed from the decision makers' personalities and their experience, from appreciation of the realities and consequences of war, and the estimates of the ability of the French economy and financial structure to support whatever decisions were made. Finally, the personal commitment of decision makers to past traditions, ideologies, or to their own expectations influenced diplomatic and military decisions. Whether realistic or otherwise, these considerations informed Louis XVI and his advisers as they pondered France's role as a great power, when they decided to engage France in war or peace, and when they deliberated on the relation between domestic and foreign policies. The decisions of their counterparts in the cabinets of Europe were influenced by similar estimates, assessments, and personal commitments.[19]

The passage to the status of a second-rate power is extraordinarily difficult for a people who have grown accustomed to the heady exercise of great power. The loss sometimes produces a fierce political reaction. Not every country is blessed with a leader who appears at the right moment, a leader—such as Charles XI of Sweden—who could lead his people "back into the grey light of everyday existence" after they had drunk the wine of victory and enormous power. Charles XI gave Sweden "policies appropriate to her resources and her real interests, equipped her to carry them out, and prepared for her a future of weight and dignity as a second-class power."[20] Louis XVI tried to give France a foreign policy appropriate to France's resources. But to many Frenchmen, there

19. Ibid., 270. An especially concise summary of Blainey's discussion is in Blanning, *The Origins of the French Revolutionary Wars*, 27–28.

20. Michael Roberts, *Essays in Swedish History* (London, 1967), 233.

was no honor or dignity whatsoever in being a second-class power, even if only temporarily, while the king reformed and regenerated France.

Thus, long-term trends in the international system combined with foreign policy decisions and political and financial disorder in France to sap the foundations of France's substantial power, to unravel its traditional diplomatic arrangements, and ultimately destroy the brief triumph of 1783. The nature and agony of France's retreat and how individual Frenchmen and Europeans responded to it is the focus of this study.

PART I

The Long and Short Term

ONE

Peace ... But

T HE YEARS between 1783 and 1789 were years of extraordinary change and uncertainty in Europe. France and England challenged each other in a naval arms race. Gustavus III of Sweden rearmed in preparation for adventures abroad
and at the same time embarked on a policy destined to create a
constitutional crisis at home. In the Dutch Republic the influence
the Patriot Party had won during the American Revolutionary
War strengthened the Patriots' determination to reduce the powers
of the Stadholder, the chief magistrate of the Dutch Republic.
Consequently, they quickened a constitutional conflict already
fraught with peril in the belief that it was the opportune moment
to consolidate their gains. Russia and Austria plotted to carve up
the Ottoman Empire while the Ottoman Turks, living on the edge
of chaos, bitterly disputed among themselves whether their decline
was the result of the failure to return to traditional ways or the failure to scrap tradition and follow Europe's military, economic, and
cultural model. There were rumors of war and there were wars: the
Prussian invasion of the Dutch Republic, a Russo-Turkish War, a
Swedish-Russian War, and the very real threat of renewed warfare
between Britain and France. Wars accelerated the remaking of the
European international system.

The Treaty of Versailles (1783) ending the American Revolutionary War was a much-needed victory for France. The signatures

on the Treaty were celebrated as signs of a victorious return, after decades of diplomatic failure, to an earlier period of French leadership in Europe. The Treaty erased in the minds of many Frenchmen the dishonorable Treaty of Paris of 1763, a treaty Louis XVI and his ministers remembered with shame and resentment, believing that Britain had imposed on France harsh and unjust terms. Moreover, the Treaty of 1783 seemingly restored France to its traditional position as arbiter of Europe and thereby accomplished a major objective of the war.[1]

Looking back on the peace of 1783, the Comte de Vergennes, Louis XVI's secretary of state for foreign affairs, placed much importance on France's triumph and assured his monarch that the victory in the American war guaranteed France's prestige as well as its security.[2] In a memoir dated 1784, he noted that France was secure. Its frontiers were established and fortified. Not one of France's continental neighbors was strong enough to threaten it. Louis XVI was free, therefore, to play the role of arbiter, to maintain the "public order" of Europe and see to it that Europe's balance of power remained stable.

The memoir also reminded the king that once Britain agreed to the independence of its former American colonies, France had accomplished all its wartime aims. To have continued that war for any other reason, Vergennes argued (against those members of Louis XVI's cabinet who had wanted to use the American war to gain additional territory for France), would have contradicted the spirit of moderation that motivated Louis XVI. In 1784, therefore,

1. Baron Pierre Victor de Besenval, *Mémoires . . . écrits par lui-même* (Paris, 1805), 3:54.

2. Unless otherwise noted, the following overview of Louis XVI's position in 1784 comes from Vergennes's "Mémoire presenté au roi, 29 March 1784," Archives des affaires étrangères-mémoires et documents-France (hereafter referred to as AAE-md-France), 587:207–25. Also printed in L. P. Ségur, L. P. Ségur, *Politique de tous les cabinets de l'Europe pendant les règnes de Louis XV et Louis XVI* (Paris, 1801), 3:196–221.

Louis XVI had good reasons to believe he had made an honorable peace, that he had exorcised the trauma of the peace of 1763 and that he had raised France, once again, to the status of arbiter of Europe.

But what did it mean to be an arbiter?

The answer that had been advanced in 1757 by Cardinal de Bernis, Louis XV's secretary of state for foreign affairs was clear: the aim of France's policies was to "play in Europe that superior role which suits its seniority, its dignity, and its grandeur."[3] Bernis's definition was not new; it was a key to the foreign policies of Louis XV's great grandfather, Louis XIV, as well as to the policies of Louis XV's grandson, Louis XVI. Indeed, for Louis XVI, the word "arbiter" along with the title "His Most Christian Majesty" defined in large part the French monarch's conception of his identity.

In the eighteenth century, Europe was largely unfamiliar with the modern practice of submitting international disputes to a tribunal for arbitration. The "arbiter" in Old Regime diplomacy was not a tribunal but an individual, a sovereign prince who helped settle international disputes by the exercise of his own power and influence, by his good offices or by mediation. When two powers were unable to settle a dispute or when they were engaged in war with each other and needed to reestablish diplomatic contacts to bring about a settlement without losing face, a neutral prince could exercise his good offices to establish a channel of communication. Also, the arbiter was sometimes played a more active role in the settlement of disputes as a mediator. He then intervened in an international dispute with substantive suggestions as to how a settlement should be reached. In doing so, he became a participant in negotiations and his international position and military power directly influenced the final settlement.

---

3. "Instructions" to the Comte de Stainville, 1757. Printed in Albert Sorel, *Recueil des Instructions données aux ambassadeurs et ministres de France . . .* (Paris, 1884), Autriche, 1:356.

Arbiters perceived their roles in many different ways. Louis XIV was never able to separate his role as arbiter from his personal determination to dominate his neighbors.[4] Moreover, his territorial ambitions made his claims as arbiter suspect, even among his allies. Nevertheless, after 1678, when the treaties of Nimwegen and Fontainebleau clearly established his international stature, Louis XIV used his military and economic power (and a good measure of personal bullying) to mediate among allies in Germany and to be the arbiter in the pacification of the Baltic. Reluctantly, statesmen recognized him as the "arbiter of Europe."[5] For Louis XIV, the title of arbiter belonged to the prince who could dominate.[6]

To be an arbiter meant something quite different to Louis XVI. He had no desire to dominate and no reckless ambition to disregard the public laws of Europe recorded in treaties. Until 1787, he consistently refused the temptation to acquire additional territory even when he had opportunities for expansion. He did so with the argument that expansion would violate the traditional balance of power. Furthermore, it was particularly important to Louis XVI's foreign policy that the princes of Europe not perceive France as a threat to their territories.[7]

The War of the American Revolution removed an important obstacle to Louis XVI's determination to be arbiter of Europe, because it left Britain with few reliable friends on the Continent. Britain had abandoned its ancient alliance with the Dutch repub-

4. Gaston Zeller, *Histoire des Relations Internationales*, vol. 3, *Les Temps Modernes; de Louis XIV à 1789* (Paris, 1955), 8.

5. Phillippe Sagnac and A. de Saint-Léger, *Louis XIV: 1661–1715* (Paris, 1949), 239.

6. Ibid., 238–62.

7. Discussions about how Louis XVI and his foreign minister Vergennes defined the role of arbiter are found in Orville T. Murphy, *Charles Gravier, Comte de Vergennes; French Diplomacy in the Age of Revolution, 1719–1787* (Albany, N.Y., 1982), 211–31; Comte de Vergennes, "Mémoire presenté au roi, 29 mars, 1784," AAE-md-France, 587:207–25.

lic and declared war on them.[8] During the war, the brutal use of British naval power against neutral shipping created a hostile international response, which even Britain could not ignore. The Armed Neutrality, led by Russia and joined by the maritime nations, was a clear signal to belligerents, especially Britain, that their naval practices were not acceptable and might, indeed, provoke an armed response. Moreover, the Armed Neutrality became a formidable barrier separating Russia from what the British considered their "natural alliance" with St. Petersburg.[9] In short, Britain was isolated.

In addition, a meeting between the Emperor Joseph II and the Russian Czarina Catherine II at Moglilev in 1780 brought Russia into secret alliance with Austria, who was, in turn, allied with France. Thus, only Prussia was left as a possible ally who could bring Britain out of isolation. But Frederick the Great, old and only a few years away from his death, was an uncertain factor. Worse still, experience had shown him to be an unreliable friend.[10]

At home, Britain faced problems demanding immediate attention. The American war left the country divided about the peace settlement and with a national debt of over £231 million.[11] A scandalous disorder in the East India Company could no longer be ignored. Ireland remained an angry and discontented land. The American war had changed Britain's position in European politics. The instructions written in the spring of 1783 to the Comte d'Adhémar, France's ambassador to London, stated as self-evident that the American war had diminished Britain's power and influence in

8. Isabel de Madariaga, *Britain, Russia and the Armed Neutrality of 1780* (New Haven, 1962), xxi, 442–47.

9. Ibid., 443–45.

10. Comte de Vergennes, "Observations sur le Coup de canon tiré sur l'Escaut, 14 November, 1784." Printed in L. P. Ségur, *Politique de tous les cabinets de l'Europe . . .* , 3:226.

11. Chris Cook and John Stevenson, *British Historical Facts, 1760–1830* (Hamden, Conn., 1980), 187.

Europe: "The Court of London, accustomed to abusing her power for nearly a century, will have some difficulty familiarizing herself with her present situation."[12]

The understandable pride Louis XVI felt about France's diplomatic accomplishments could not, however, exorcise the many threats to the tranquillity of Europe. While France was engaged in the American Revolutionary War, the settlement at the Peace of Kainardji (1774) between Russia and the Ottoman Empire fell apart. The "unbelievable weakness" of the Turkish Empire was no secret, and it sorely tested the self-control of the Turks' neighbors. The alliance of Joseph II of Austria and Catherine II fostered the suspicion that the two rulers were plotting to surrender to temptation: there would be further spoliation of the Turks. In June of 1782, Tartars in the Crimea revolted against their kahn. Because the Tartars' kahn was a puppet of Catherine II, the rebellion could hardly remain a domestic squabble. The Turks suggested a commission of inquiry to deal with the Crimean problem. Catherine refused. Instead, she presented an ultimatum to the Turks, invaded the Crimea, and restored the Kahn to power. To demonstrate his support of Catherine, Joseph II ordered troops to the Ottoman frontier.

France had encouraged the Turks to declare war in the previous conflict between the Turks and Russia; because Catherine remembered the past, she was little inclined to trust Versailles in her new situation. So it was Joseph II who asked Louis XVI to join with him to persuade the Turks to accept the Russian demands on them. Louis agreed, but soon found himself the dupe of Russian ambitions. Catherine annexed the territory she had occupied and left to Joseph II the task of explaining it all to his brother-in-law, the king of France. When Joseph did so, he insinuated to France

12. "Mémoire pour servir d'instruction au sieur Comte d'Adhémar . . . allant en Angleterre en qualité d'ambassadeur . . . , 25 April, 1783," printed in Paul Vaucher, ed., *Recueil des Instructions aux ambassadeurs et ministres de France* . . .(Paris, 1965), vol. XXV, tome 3, 514–15.

that he did not approve of Catherine's actions. Yet his engagements with her, he complained, made it impossible to oppose her openly. Joseph had no choice, he believed, but to make the best of the opportunity and find compensation for himself at the expense of the Turks. He expected his Bourbon ally to support him or, at least, to remain silent.

Louis XVI did neither. Russia's aggrandizement was deplorable and certainly of long-term concern to France. But Austrian aggrandizement at the expense of the Turks' European provinces constituted a direct and immediate threat to France. Louis would have none of it and made his position clear to Joseph. He assured Joseph of his strong attachment to Austria, but he reminded him that the fundamental assumption of the French-Austrian alliance was the preservation of the territories of the member states of Europe. To France, the Ottoman Empire was a part of Europe.

Louis's response offended Joseph. It was, he thought, excessively moral and legalistic. But he realized that Louis XVI would not be persuaded to change his mind, so he turned about and denied ever having had designs on the Turks. Eventually the Turks, under pressure from France as well as Britain and Austria, reluctantly agreed to the Russian annexation of the Crimea.

But the settlement between the Turks and the Russians did not produce calm in Europe. Every power in the north of Europe was rearming. Never before in peacetime had relations among powers in the Baltic been so agitated, Vergennes noted in 1784.[13]

And there were other threats to peace. Versailles suspected that Joseph II might use his Russian support to attack powers other than the Ottoman Empire. A recent trip by Joseph to Naples had provided circumstantial evidence that Joseph was, indeed, plotting something in Italy. On the other hand, perhaps Joseph would strike his long-time enemy Frederick II of Prussia. What happened to Prussia was one of the keys to whether Europe would

---

13. "Vergennes to Pons, 4 July 1784," Archives des affaires étrangères-correspondance politique-Suède (hereafter referred to as AAE-cp-Suède), 276:158vo.

have war or peace. In the memoir of 1784, Vergennes stressed that Joseph II was forever searching for ways to weaken Frederick II. The Austrians could not forgive the king of Prussia for annexing Austria's former territory of Silesia. Observers in Versailles believed that Joseph II still wanted to regain Silesia, by force if necessary. That ambition was a principal reason why Austria allied with France. Hostility toward Prussia tied Austria to France. France's interest required, therefore, that Prussian power not be diminished. If it were, Vergennes warned, Austria would soon return to its "old system," an alliance with Britain.

Louis XVI knew that whatever diplomatic success France enjoyed in Germany in the first ten years of his reign was partially due to France's ability to play off Prussian power against Austrian. Frederick II, too, recognized his importance as the "counterweight" to Austria.[14] In the German Empire, the role of counterweight was especially useful to him when he played the role of defender of the smaller states. Of course, this delicate but effective balance could easily crumble. If Prussia allied with Britain, France could no longer hold the balance between Prussia and Austria. If Prussia turned eastward and cemented a relation with St. Petersburg and Vienna as it had done in the First Partition of Poland (1772), France would be effectively blocked in Eastern Europe, reduced, according to one contemporary observer, to the level of a second-rate power.[15]

No matter how one calculated the values, Prussia's growing strength and influence in Europe could not be ignored. The First Partition of Poland left Prussia with a piece of Polish territory of great commercial and maritime value. In the Baltic, Prussia was now a power to reckon with. Britain had the naval power, certainly,

14. J. G. Droysen, et al., eds., *Politische Correspondenz Friedrich des Grossen* (Leipzig, 1931), 42:420.

15. M. Favier, "Conjectures raisonnées sur la situation actuelle de la France dans le système politique de l'Europe . . . ," in L. P. Ségur, *Politique de tous les cabinets . . . ,* 1:251, 235, 483.

to bring Prussia to heel in the Baltic Sea, but had to respect Prussian power because King George III's electorate of Hanover was vulnerable to land invasion by Prussian soldiers. Frederick II was a difficult personality to deal with, but the importance of Prussia was not a question of a person, Vergennes wrote in 1784: "The man will pass, the power will remain"; France needed a friendly Prussian power if Louis XVI was to exercise his role as arbiter.

Vergennes insisted, however, that his attitude toward Prussia did not imply that he wished France to weaken its ties with Austria. "Nothing could be further from my thoughts," he assured his monarch. But Joseph II's aggressive personality, his obvious ambitions, and his expectations that Marie Antoinette, his sister, would arrange things in his favor at Versailles, made French statesmen uneasy that the House of Austria would launch some adventure that would harm French interests and violate Louis XVI's "sense of justice."[16] Thus, France's international position after the American Revolutionary War depended heavily on keeping Prussia in the French orbit and Austria contained. A strong, but not too strong, Prussia was the critical counterweight to Austria.

A stern warning concluded Vergennes's 1784 memoir: France must look to strengthening its military power. That was the surest way to keep the respect of others. But to exercise power, Vergennes told his king, Louis XVI had to keep his finances in good order. Healthy finances were essential to the maintenance of an effective army and navy. Especially, Vergennes urged, keep the navy strong. "It is the only real security Your Majesty has for an enduring peace with England." The British were rebuilding their navy, Vergennes warned, and it would soon be stronger than it was at the moment of peace. Furthermore, Britain forever watched for a chance to avenge the settlement that closed the American War. It would be difficult to imagine a long peace, Vergennes said, if France was unable to

16. Vergennes's "Mémoire au Roi, March 29, 1784," 207–25; L. P. Ségur, *Politique de tous les cabinets . . .* , 3:214–15.

maintain others' respect. "Placed in the center of Europe, . . .
[France] seems destined to calm the waves of ambition. Do not
lose sight, Sire, of this superb prerogative. What more glorious use
could Your Majesty make of his power than . . . to make justice and
concord reign in Europe!"[17]

17. Ibid., 218.

TWO

Diplomacy and Paying for War

"WAR," according to the Prussian General Helmut von Molkte, "is a necessary part of God's arrangement of the world." His theology may have been flawed; his history was not. Fiercely competitive, the international system of the eighteenth century bred war.[1] And no matter how a monarch of a great power conceived of his role in that system, wars or threats of war were ever present. The system created enormous military demands. Perhaps the sixteenth and seventeenth centuries showed a higher frequency of war, but eighteenth-century wars involved more men and were, generally, more demanding on the resources of the countries involved. Furthermore, the wars became more intense and more worldwide as the century progressed. Unfortunately, France fought in a great number of these wars.[2]

To make war, princes had at their command permanent standing armies and navies owned, equipped, and supplied by the crown. As the population, wealth, and level of political organization of the state grew in the late seventeenth century, military numbers also grew. The size of European armies increased fivefold

1. Quincy Wright, *A Study of War* (Chicago, 1964),53; Jack S. Levy, *War in the Modern Great Power System, 1495–1975* (Lexington, Ky., 1983), 3.

2. The empirical studies on which these statements are based are Quincy Wright, *Study of War*, 51–54, and Jack S. Levy, *War in the Modern Great Power System*, 1–7, 77–149.

between 1600 and 1760.[3] Louis XVI's foreign policy required the building and maintenance of a large navy.[4] But shipbuilding in France was especially dear. France paid more, ship for ship, than did Britain. A ship built in Sweden cost only two-fifths what the same ship cost in France.[5] In *The Wealth of Nations*, Adam Smith noted how the costs of maintaining military establishments and providing them with modern arms and ammunition had swollen in his century. Only the nation that could afford the expense, he observed, would enjoy the military advantage.[6] To make war and pay for armaments to sustain diplomacy you must have money.[7] In

3. Geoffrey Parker, "The Military Revolution, 1560–1660—A Myth?" *Journal of Modern History* 48, no. 2 (June 1976), 206–11; Christopher Lloyd and J. R. Western, "Armed Forces and the Art of War," in A. Goodwin, ed., *The New Cambridge Modern History* (Cambridge, England, 1965), 8:186, 190; Georges Livet and Roland Mousnier, *Histoire générale de l'Europe* (Paris, 1980), 2:566; between 1781 and 1790, the budgeted strength of the French army fluctuated between 266,000 and 282,603 men. The question of whether or not the cost of the individual soldier *in France* increased or decreased is still a matter of discussion. Claude C. Sturgill, in his study "Observations of the French War Budget, 1781–1790," *Military Affairs* 48, no. 3 (October 1984), 180–87, argues that the money spent to support the individual soldier actually decreased. The budget of 1720 averages about 567 livres per man, while the budget of 1790 allotes only 374 livres per man. Using the same formula, the budget of 1781 spent 376 livres per man. But Sturgill says (184) that the 268,784 strength of the army in 1781 "existed largely on paper. . . . [T]he real army of 1781 totalled only 172,104." If this was the case, France budgeted 588 livres per soldier in 1781. In his article "Recalculating French Army Growth during the *Grand Siècle*, 1610–1750," *French Historical Studies* 18, no. 4 (Fall 1994), 881–906, John A. Lynn, using as a base line the years 1494–1610, estimates that the French wartime army by the end of the seventeenth century grew by 400–700 percent. Equally significant for state budgets are his estimates that the peacetime numbers for this period grew by an amazing 650–1500 percent (p. 903).

4. Jonathan R. Dull, *The French Navy and American Independence* (Princeton, 1975), xi, 56–65.

5. Douglas Dakin, *Turgot And the Ancien Régime in France* (New York, 1965), 127.

6. See his discussion "Of the Expence of Defence," in *The Wealth of Nations* (New York: Modern Library, 1967), 653–69.

7. Albert Sorel, *L'Europe et la Révolution Française* (Paris, 1885), 1:303.

1773, just before the accession of Louis XVI, the French diplomatic agent Favier was asked to prepare a memoir on France's position in Europe. Favier was asked to review, for the benefit of the incoming king, the three fundamentals of diplomatic influence: military power, power derived from alliances and relations, and power derived from financial means. It is prophetically symbolic that Favier never finished part three.[8]

Early in the eighteenth century, Louis XV's first minister, the Cardinal de Fleury, recognized the disruptive effects of war on France and managed, for a while at least, to keep the peace. He made no attempt to significantly reform the fiscal or financial system, but because France managed to avoid major wars and enjoyed a modest prosperity, the financial structure of the monarchy was not subjected to excessive pressures.[9] In fact, the perseverance of Fleury and his controller general of finances, Orry, resulted in one of the few periods in eighteenth-century French financial history when revenues and expenditures were in near equilibrium.[10] But Fleury had his critics. They saw his policies as timid and unheroic, unsuited to the status of a great power. Nevertheless, he provided France with a much-needed respite and, consequently, the time to recover from the financial chaos, debts, and economic damages left behind after the death of Louis XIV.[11] When France entered the War of the Austrian Succession in 1740, however, the period of recuperation came to a close.

Between 1726 and 1789 the ordinary military budgets of France grew more than two and one-half times.[12] French monarchs relied

8. L. P. Ségur, *Politique de tous les cabinets de l'Europe* (Paris, 1793), 1:144–45.

9. Alfred Cobban, *A History of Modern France* (Baltimore, 1961), 1:29, 32–37.

10. René Stourm, *Les Finances de l'Ancien Régime et de la Révolution* (Paris, 1885), 1:17–19. Michel Morineau, "Budgets de l'état et gestion des finances royales en France au dix-huitième siècle," *Revue historique* 264, no. 2, (Oct.-Dec. 1980), 304.

11. Derek Jarrett, *The Begetters of Revolution* (Totowa, N.J., 1973), 105; Alfred Cobban, *A History of Modern France* 1:32–34.

12. Michel Morineau, "Budgets de l'état," 317.

on a variety of ways to pay their bills: direct and indirect taxes, lotteries, life annuities, loans and anticipations from officials and institutions, and loans from domestic and foreign money-markets —even disguised bankruptcies.[13] Until the later decades of the eighteenth century, the treasury of France also made an effort to pay for war by raising taxes.[14]

But the Seven Years' War as well as the American Revolutionary War (1778–83) represented a departure in the history of eighteenth-century French finances. In both cases, the French government decided to fund the major costs of war with loans without increasing taxes to cover the additional costs of servicing such loans. Before the Seven Years' War, the French treasury spent about 30 percent of revenues on debt service, consisting mostly of interest payments. After the war and up to the eve of the Revolution, debt service reached 50 percent of revenues. This departure imposed crippling burdens on the financial system. In addition, for the use of money from loans, the French monarchy paid dearly.

The monarchy sold offices to raise money. Wealthy men bought government offices, even the posts of treasurer of departments. A treasurer of the navy, for example, obtained his office not necessarily because of his administrative abilities, but because he had, or had access to, money. He was expected to manage the ordinary funds of the department and find extra funds to meet extraordinary expenditures. The treasurer, in turn, used departmental moneys for his own private investments or loans. The conflicts of interest inherent in such practices were usually ignored, though not always, for the legality of the treasurer's use of public money for personal profits was ambiguous. Unfortunately for the well being of French finances, these officers were also acutely vulnerable to

13. Jean Bouvier and Germain-Martin, *Finances et Financiers de l'Ancien Régime* (Paris, 1969), 96.

14. James C. Riley, "French Finances, 1727–1768," *Journal of Modern History* 59 (June 1987): 236.

economic crises, especially the depression that struck France in the 1780s.[15]

After major wars the French government frequently established *chambres de justice* to review the activities of government officials as well as the activities of businesses supplying goods and services to the war. The declared aim was to find and punish corruption or profiteering. But the trials and convictions of the individuals became convenient ways to explain away poor military performance and evade the issue of the high costs of war. Above all, the attention and publicity given to the trials made it possible to avoid reexamining questionable decisions about international politics and military strategies. Thus, the trials shifted scrutiny away from the government and its policies and placed the blame for extravagances and failures on the shoulders of corrupt individuals.

In addition, the *chambres de justice* helped the state pay its bills. The government often confiscated the wealth of convicted officials and refused to pay full value on their credit notes. Consequently, these individuals not only became scapegoats but also provided an effective way to cut the war debt. After the disastrous Seven Years' War the French government created the famous Fontanieu Commission to review the costs of the navy and colonies and eventually to look into the costs of the war in Canada.[16] The commission questioned the legitimacy of some naval debts and the entire Canadian war debt. Corruption, it was alleged, had caused both military defeats and the huge debts. Consequently, the government stopped payment on those debts it decided were questionable and refused to pay full value on others. What was left of the short-term debt incurred during the war was deferred and converted into

15. See, for example, the career of Claude Baudard de Sainte-James in Denise Ozanam, *Claude Baudard de Sainte-James: trésorier général de la Marine et Brasseur d'Affaires (1738–1787)* (Geneva, 1969). Baudard was wiped out by the crisis of the 1780s.

16. J. F. Bosher, "The French Government's Motives in the Affaire du Canada, 1761–1763," *English Historical Review* 96, no. 378 (January 1981), 70.

long-term or funded debts with low rates of interest. The Canadian debts were redeemed at one-half their value and converted into bonds paying only 4 percent.[17] This was disguised bankruptcy.

But was corruption the major or only problem? Frenchmen of the Old Régime could not agree and neither have historians since. Fortunately, some excellent studies now available have begun to clarify the picture. There is general agreement that France was a wealthy country, rich in population and resources, and French ministers knew the value of France's potential wealth.[18] Furthermore, there is some agreement that Frenchmen, generally, did not pay more taxes to the central government then did taxpayers elsewhere. In fact, in the latter part of the eighteenth century, France may have been become "something of a tax haven."[19] A comparative study of the incidence of taxation in Britain and in France indicates that the ordinary Englishmen actually carried a heavier tax burden from the central government than did Frenchmen.[20] Why, then, did France have so much difficulty paying its bills? Was the fiscal and financial administration of France fatally flawed, making failure an inevitable outcome?

One view holds that both Britain and France carried heavy charges on debt servicing, but the British had the advantage of having more control over financing and accounting.[21] The French

17. Ibid., 75–76.

18. Baron Pierre Victor de Besenval, *Mémoires . . . écrits par lui-même* (Paris, 1805), 3:231; M. Favier, "Conjectures raisonnés sur la situation actuelle de la France dans le système politique de l'Europe . . ." in L. P. Ségur, *Politique de tous les cabinets de l'Europe . . .* , 1:424; *Cambridge Modern History*, 8:70, 222.

19. Riley, "French Finances," 237.

20. Peter Mathias and Patrick O'Brien, "Taxation in Britain and France, 1715–1810. A Comparison of the Social and Economic Incidence of Taxes Collected by the Central Governments," *European Economic History Review* 33 (1980): 601–50; Derek Jarrett, *The Begetters of Revolution*, 24.

21. J. F. Bosher, "Current Writings on Administration and Finance in 18th-Century France," *Journal of Modern History* 53 (March 1981): 80; J. F. Bosher, *French Finances, 1770–1785: From Business to Bureaucracy* (Cambridge, 1970), 24; James C. Riley, *International Government Finance and the Amsterdam Capital Market: 1740–1815* (Cambridge, 1980), 125.

government, according to this interpretation, had limited knowledge of or control over its own finances because they were, for the most part, managed by officials who had purchased their offices and were not fully accountable to the government. The system was a form of private enterprise and the officers' relations with the crown were contractual, which made it difficult for the king to control them. J. F. Bosher described the system as a "bottomless pit capable of absorbing almost any amount of revenue."[22] The growing deficits, he contends, were symptoms of major institutional dysfunction, and these defects inevitably drove up the overhead costs of financing the state.[23] The recurring unbalanced budgets and the conflicts over taxes were, therefore, simply derivative problems.[24] The reforms of Jacques Necker (the Swiss banker and Louis XVI's director of finances), which included among other things the elimination of some of the venal offices of intendants of finance, were thus important and necessary attempts to render financial administration more efficient and more accountable.[25]

And there is additional evidence to add to the picture of inefficiency. When the French government farmed out tax collection by negotiating loan-leases with the company of general farms every six years, the contracts were based on economic statistics that were sometimes as much as four years out of date. In the expanding economy of most of the eighteenth century, this meant that in times of prosperity the company of general farms, and not the French government, benefited most from increased tax yields. The system of the general farms, therefore, did not provide the state with revenues that grew at the same pace as the economy.[26] Rev-

22. Bosher, *French Finances*, xi.

23. Bosher, "Current Writings," 80.　　24. Ibid.

25. The nature and value of Necker's reforms are discussed in detail in Robert D. Harris, *Necker, Reform Statesman of the Ancien Régime* (Berkeley, 1979) and J. F. Bosher, *French Finances*, 142–65.

26. George T. Matthews, *The Royal General Farms in Eighteenth-Century France* (New York, 1958), 266.

enue collection by the general farms also meant that costs of collection of taxes reached about 13 percent of revenues after the mid-eighteenth century. More stringent limits on general farms profits might have reduced collection costs to about 9 percent. But one historian insists that the controller generals did not always "grasp the issues clearly or well."[27]

Structural inefficiency and incompetence at the top of Old Regime France surely were important factors in the financial crisis that Louis XVI faced in 1786–87. Nevertheless, these defects fail to provide the full explanation for the breakdown of French finances on the eve of the Revolution. James Riley, in fact, concludes that "neither more efficiency in assessing revenues, nor more efficiency in administering collections and expenditures would have saved the monarchy." The real problem was the burden of debt and the great imbalance between revenue and debt.[28]

After mid-century the French monarch became increasingly reluctant to repudiate loans or to use partial bankruptcy as a way of reducing the debt. The reactions of public opinion to ministerial decisions about finances had to be taken into consideration by the monarch and his ministers because the investing public had become more sophisticated about where it placed its money.[29] "Creditors," Benjamin Franklin observed, "have better memories than debtors." This characteristic of money lenders no doubt restrained a finance minister who contemplated repudiating or changing the terms of a loan. And we must not forget that there were ministers, such as Necker, and a monarch, such as Louis XVI, whose personal moral sense did not permit the violation of the trust and confidence involved in loans and debts.

27. James C. Riley, *The Seven Years' War and the Old Regime in France: The Economic and Financial Toll* (Princeton, 1986), 161–62.

28. Riley, "Dutch Investments in France, 1781–1787," *Journal of Economic History* 33, no. 4 (December 1973), 738.

29. George Alter and James C. Riley, "How to Bet on Lives: A Guide to Life Contingent Contracts in Early Modern Europe," *Research in Economic History* 10 (1986) ed. Paul Uselding, 37–38.

As the eighteenth century drew to a close, France turned more and more, as did other European states, to the international money markets of Europe to borrow and pay expenses.[30] It was a way of avoiding the unpopular alternative of higher taxes and it shifted the costs of war and foreign policy to future generations. In addition, for reasons not altogether clear, French borrowers consistently paid higher rates for money than did other major powers.[31] France sometimes used a loan instrument, the life annuity, which was especially costly.[32] Historians continue to debate how much more France paid for loans than did other powers. But certainly France paid more for loans than was necessary.[33] In the 1780s there was a borrower's market. Amsterdam had an oversupply of capital and was, therefore, "biased" in favor of the borrower.[34]

The obvious solution to the public debt in France was higher taxes, but they created universal public resentment. Taxes were more visible in France than in Britain, and the Frenchman saw the tax collector as a threat to his rights of privacy. Urban dwellers probably paid more taxes to the central government than others and in cities, especially Paris, opposition to taxes easily merged with a long and vigorous tradition of rebellion.[35] Also, the poverty of the state reflected, in part, the poverty of the rural masses.[36] In the rural countryside, a large segment of the French population was poor. In the later decades of the eighteenth century, an economic depression and a rapid rise in some prices intensified pauperization and destitution. Under such circumstances, increased taxes were not just a burden, they became an oppression. Resentment over increased taxation inflamed public opinion and easily

30. George V. Taylor, "The Paris Bourse on the Eve of the French Revolution, 1781–1789," *American Historical Review* 67 (1961–62): 953.

31. Riley, *International Government Finance*, 110, 158, 176.

32. Alter and Riley, "How to Bet on Lives," 26, 28.

33. Riley, *International Government Finance*, 110, 174.

34. Ibid., 41; Riley, "Dutch Investment in France, 1781–1787," 735.

35. Michel Morineau, "Budgets de l'état," 322.

36. Bouvier and Germain-Martin, *Finances et Financiers de l'Ancien Régime*, 99.

turned into political conflict. Differences about who should pay as well as who should decide who pays sparked bitter disputes among the literate public, among French ministers, among nobles, the Parlement and the Assembly of Notables. Unavoidably, questions about taxes and finances became politicized. Out of these quarrels, in the late 1780s, grew the loosely formed French Patriot party and the Society of Thirty. Such political groups would provide leadership in the revolutionary crisis of the winter of 1788 and spring of 1789.[37]

But there was another reason why French tax revenues did not grow at the same rate as the expanding economy and did not pay for the increasing costs of war. "The scale of [tax] evasion was massive. . . ." Frenchmen would not provide their government with information essential to estimating income levels. Whenever the government tried to take a census or assess property values, it met a stone wall of popular and legal resistance. The government's inability or lack of political will to tax, therefore, must be added to the reasons why it was impossible for France to reap the benefits of revenues tied to economic expansion.[38] When economic expansion itself began to decline after 1770, the tax base could no longer carry the burden of great-power status. The problem was not, as Necker's critics argued, that war was financed by loans. Even more than France, Britain financed its wars with loans. But after the American Revolutionary War, William Pitt raised taxes to pay for the loans. France increased taxes, but not enough to pay for the loans. Louis XVI's contemporary, the baron de Besenval, recognized that taxes were much resented in France. But he also recognized that Louis had to have more revenue if he wished to avoid bankruptcy. If necessary, Besenval insisted, the king must use his soldiers to follow the tax collector to see to it that taxes were col-

37. Daniel L. Wick, *A Conspiracy of Well-Intentioned Men: The Society of Thirty and the French Revolution* (New York, 1987), 333.

38. James C. Riley, *The Seven Years' War*, 70.

lected.[39] "The time for patience and negotiation is past," Besenval wrote to the keeper of the seal, "each day serves only to diminish the authority of the king."[40] Louis's inability to find tax revenues left him face to face with a devastating financial crisis. He might have saved his head, Michel Morineau observed, if he had only raised taxes high enough.[41]

But Morineau's analysis goes further. He does not believe there was a "tragic failure" of the financial administration of France.[42] The routine performance of the French financial administration failed only when war brought huge, unanticipated expenses and at the same time diminished revenues from certain indirect taxes, such as customs duties on foreign commerce.[43] War made it very difficult, if not impossible, to control spending or even account for money spent. Thus, the fundamental sources of France's financial and political crises were badly conceived foreign policies, frequent wars, and the runaway expenses they entailed. Morineau insists: "War, foreign policy decisions," were the primary causes of the "financial shipwreck" of France.[44]

Surely, the cost of great-power status might have been less damaging to France if the government had achieved greater control over its financial administration and accounting. If French ministers had learned how to tap with higher taxes the growing wealth

39. Besenval, *Mémoires*, 3:235.   40. Ibid., 3:231.

41. Michel Morineau, "Budgets de l'état," 327.

42. Françoise Mosser concurs. She even maintains that Necker's reforms were unnecessary; in fact, they harmed. The officers Necker dismissed in his reforms were capable and honest men who were needed in the administration: Françoise Mosser, *Les Intendants des finances au XVIIIe siècle* (Paris, 1978), 249.

43. Fernand Braudel and Ernest Labrousse, *Histoire économique et sociale de la France* (Paris, 1970), 2:554–66; Robert D. Harris, "Necker's Compte rendu of 1781: A Reconsideration," *Journal of Modern History* 42, no. 2 (June 1970), 180.

44. Michel Morineau, "Budgets de l'état," 317; See also Alain Guéry, "Les finances de la monarchie française sous l'Ancien Régime," *Annales: E.S.C.* 33, no. 2 (March-April 1978), 227.

of France and better exploit the international capital markets, France might have remained solvent. It is certainly arguable that if Louis XVI and his ministers had had the political persistence and abilities to reform the government and make the reforms stick, France might have survived its revolutionary crisis. But major, long-term reforms would have taken years to complete, and long-term reforms were difficult to undertake during wartime or in peacetime when major preparations for war were underway. Unfortunately, France was too often at war, or trying to get out from under the burden of a recent war, or preparing for another war to provide the environment for long-term reform. Thus, one of the most serious problems Louis XVI faced during the last decades of the 1780s was the chronic inability of the French financial system to pay for France's great-power status, to underwrite the frequent wars and finance the French monarch's desire to be arbiter of Europe. The French fiscal and financial system needed a reprieve, a disengagement, to recover. In short, it needed peace. But no sooner was the Seven Years' War settled, than preparations for the next war began.[45] The fireworks celebrations of the end of the American Revolutionary War had scarcely gone out before French accepted the challenge of a naval arms race with Britain.[46]

By 1787 accounts of the French treasury show expenditures of 629 million livres, with an income of only 503 million livres. Twenty-six percent of the expenditures were devoted to the cost of the military and fifty-one percent of expenditures were earmarked for interests or charges on the debts, debts incurred largely to pay for war and foreign affairs. While many contemporaries blamed the deficits on court extravagances and lush pensions for favorites (and, indeed, these costs amounted to about six percent of the budget) the numbers are compelling: more than seventy-five percent of the budget

45. Derek Jarrett, *The Begetters of Revolution*, 70–71.
46. Jeremy Black, "Sir Robert Ainslie: His Majesty's Agent-provocateur? British Foreign Policy and the International Crisis of 1787," *European History Quarterly* 14 (1984): 259.

was consumed by debt service, other charges for loans, the military services, and the Department of Foreign Affairs. These were the costs of maintaining France's great-power position in Europe.[47]

In 1787, financiers who had been administering and providing for the state's shaky finances began to go bankrupt—five of them, in fact. They were victims of a credit crisis generated by the collapse of a speculative boom and an economic recession that had settled over France. They were unable to raise the money they needed to meet their commitments. The state was now face to face with bankruptcy.[48] In 1788, a contemporary observer, the comte de Ferrand, later remembered, "The treasury was empty. [The minister] Loménie [de Brienne], without plans or resources, proposed, in the month of August, several miserable solutions which were only bankruptcy in disguise."[49] The consequences for the Department of Foreign Affairs was a disastrous budget cut. Prepared in November of 1788, the budget for foreign affairs suffered a forty-two percent retrenchment. Among other things, all subsidies to foreign powers, especially the huge ones to Sweden, were either cut altogether or suspended for that year. Louis XVI could no longer afford the stakes of the game he had played in international politics since 1774.[50]

47. Michel Vovelle, *The Fall of the French Monarchy: 1788–1792*, trans. Susan Burke (Cambridge, 1984), 75–76.

48. See George V. Taylor's review of J. F. Bosher's *French Finances, 1770–1795*, in *Journal of Economic History* 31 (1971): 949–53.

49. Comte de Ferrand, *Mémoires du Comte de Ferrand, ministre d'Etat sous Louis XVII*, publiés pour la Société d'Histoire Contemporaine par le Vicomte de Broc. (Paris, 1897), 13:26.

50. "Project des fonds à régler pour le service des Affaires Etrangères pendant l'année 1789," Archives Diplomatique, Nantes, Series: Comptabilité, carton 63.

THREE

Long-term Transformations: Europe

ALONG WITH his growing financial problems, Louis XVI faced serious diplomatic problems resulting from long-term but steady transformations of the European state system. The growth of Britain's potential power in Europe and the world kept pace with its enormous commercial and economic development and its powerful navy. By the end of the seventeenth century, Britain had positioned itself for the role as "balancer" in Europe's balance of power, a role it would continue to exercise with considerable authority until the twentieth century. On the eastern periphery of Europe, Russia continued in the eighteenth century a dramatic rise to power, begun in the seventeenth but accelerated by Catherine II (the Great), "one of the most remarkable and successful rulers of her generation."[1] Catherine's ability to exploit her power and take advantage of the weaknesses of others both startled and awed European statesmen, some of whom still could not even bring themselves to consider Russia a part of the European international system.

But after mid-eighteenth century, the Russian presence in Eu-

1. Richard Lodge, "The European Powers and the Eastern Question," in Lord Acton, ed., *The Cambridge Modern History* (London, 1908), 8:307. Twentieth-century historians have recognized Catherine's extraordinary talents. See, for example, Isabel de Madariaga, *Britain, Russia and the Armed Neutrality of 1780* (New Haven, 1962), 441–46, 454–57.

rope could not be denied. Russia's export trade in the Baltic flourished and the Russian merchant fleet grew.[2] Using experienced foreign officers to make up for Russia's shortage of trained naval officers, Catherine developed a navy with the capacity to protect the fast-growing Russian merchant fleet.[3] As in the north, Russia's military presence expanded in the south. In the war with the Ottoman Empire from 1768 to 1774, Catherine emerged with a settlement that forced the Turks to permit Russian ships to navigate freely in the Black Sea. Russia entered the Ottoman market and soon had captured the iron market from Britain and begun to replace the British Levant Company in the fur trade.[4]

Russia's menacing expansion southward, which the Turk's were obviously unable to resist, directly threatened France's commercial interests as well as its diplomatic role in the Ottoman Empire and Eastern Europe.[5] Behind the Franco-Russian commercial treaty of 1787 was the vain French hope that France and Russia could reach an accommodation that would halt depredations on the Ottoman Empire and protect the French Levant trade.

During the Bavarian Succession War (1778–79) between Prussia and Austria, Catherine was Louis XVI's co-mediator to restore to the elector palatinate, Karl Theodor, the Bavarian territory that had been partitioned and partly annexed by Joseph II. When the Treaty of Teschen (1779) settled the conflict, she stood alongside

2. M. Favier, "Conjectures Raisonnées sur la situation actuelle de la France dans le système politique de l'Europe," in L. P. Ségur, *Politique de tous les cabinets de l'Europe* (Paris, 1801), 1:269–72, 336–37; Madariaga, *Armed Neutrality*, 443.

3. Jan Glete, "Sails and Oars, Warships and Navies in the Baltic During the 18th Century (1700–1815)," in Martine Acerra, José Merino, and Jean Meyer, eds., *Les Marines de Guerre Européennes XVII–XVIIIe siècles* (Paris, 1985), 374; Christopher Lloyd, "Armed Forces and the Art of War," in A. Goodwin, ed., *The New Cambridge Modern History* (Cambridge, 1965) 189–90. See also: M. S. Anderson, "Great Britain and the Growth of the Russian Navy," *Mariner's Mirror*, May 1956.

4. William Hale and Ali Ihsan Bagis, eds., *Four Centuries of Turco-British Relations* (North Yorkshire, 1984), 41; Jan Glete, "Sails and Oars," 385.

5. Ibid., 306–7.

Louis XVI and Frederick the Great as a staunch defender of the small powers of Germany.[6] In so doing, she forced Louis XVI to share with her the role of arbiter and protector of the Treaties of Westphalia. In the War of the American Revolution, her resolute insistence on armed neutrality once again confirmed her increasing influence in European affairs. At the same time, with the Franco-Russian commercial treaty of 1787 Russia effectively emancipated itself from the dominance Britain had exercised for so long over Russia's foreign trade.[7] During meetings and secret agreements with Joseph II in 1780, Catherine sketched grandiose plans for the partition of the Ottoman Empire.[8] By the end of the American War the annexation of the Crimea was nearly complete. The Treaty of Constantinople in 1784 translated the annexation into public law.

Catherine was an imposing personality in Europe and a self-appointed mediator in European affairs. Between Austria and Prussia, neither of whom had been able to gain an advantage over the other in the Bavarian Succession War, she held the balance of power and could play off one against the other.[9] She was in an excellent position to exploit the differences between Great Britain and France.[10] And her obvious designs on the Ottoman Empire threatened long-established French commercial interests there, and also threatened to change the balance of power in Eastern Europe in a way destined to reduce France's influence. Russia's place and reputation in Europe also meant that it now had access to Europe's money markets to finance war and diplomacy.[11]

6. Murphy, *Charles Gravier, Comte de Vergennes: French Diplomacy in the Age of Revolution, 1719–1787* (Albany, N.Y., 1982), 306–11.

7. Madariaga, *Armed Neutrality*, 442–43, 458.

8. Murphy, *Vergennes*, 312–20.

9. On the approximate equality of Austria and Prussia, see Harold Temperley, *Frederic the Great and Kaiser Joseph* (London, 1915), 113–50.

10. Madariaga, *Armed Neutrality*, 441–42; Richard Lodge, "The European Powers and the Eastern Question," 308.

11. James C. Riley, *International Government Finance and the Amsterdam Capital Market: 1740–1815* (Cambridge, 1980), 158.

While the Russian Empire slowly forced its way into the European community of great powers, France's relative power declined. Louis XVI's triumph in the American Revolutionary War proved to be a flash in the pan. In fact, the very *éclat* of the success created the response that subverted it. Awakened to the reality of defeat and isolation, Britons reacted. In December of 1783, the year the Treaty of Versailles was concluded, William Pitt became the first commissioner of the British treasury.[12] He had to deal first with the financial confusion created by the war, but gradually he began to build, along with George III, the foreign secretary, Carmarthen, and several energetic diplomats, Britain's return to the Continent.

The first indications that Britain was breaking out of its postwar isolation occurred in Denmark, where foreign policy during the war (at least as London saw it) had fallen totally under the influence of St. Petersburg.[13] Early in 1784, the young Crown Prince Frederick of Denmark, just sixteen and constitutionally able to participate in the government, surprised his family and the members of the government with a political coup, which placed men of his choice on the governing council. He ended the coup with a decree that all orders in council henceforth required his countersignature. Among the supporters of this maneuver was the British diplomat Hugh Elliot, one of the most dramatic personalities of eighteenth-century diplomacy.

Elliot had been recalled from his post as British representative to Prussia because the king of Prussia found him "disagreeable." In the winter of 1782 London sent him to Copenhagen to represent George III there. Elliot was a curious individual. At one time contemplating suicide, at another time deeply in love with his "Miss Cabbage," always in debt, a gambler who loved to place bets on the outcome of battles if there were British generals or admirals involved, it was Elliot who helped plan for the prince royal's politi-

12. Robin Reilly, *William Pitt the Younger* (London, 1978), 118.

13. Stormont to Morton Eden, December 28, 1781; in James F. Chance, ed., *British Diplomatic Instructions* (London, 1926), Denmark, 3:208.

cal coup. He worked with Count Bernstorff, who was soon to be the Danish first minister.[14] "For my part, I have thought myself under the necessity of taking a decision without waiting for any instructions from home, as there was no possibility of their arriving before the conclusion of this important transaction," Elliot wrote to his superiors in London. Fortunately, the presence of several British ships in the Copenhagen harbor provided him with what he called "essential assistance," in case those opposed to the prince royal's actions resorted to an "overt act of violence."[15]

Though the influence of Russia over Danish policy was by no means destroyed, Hugh Elliot was now well placed to influence decisions in Denmark as well as diplomatic affairs in the Baltic. And, as we shall see, he did so with vigor during the Russo-Swedish war of 1788. Pleased with Elliot's achievement in bringing the young prince royal and the Count Bernstorff into power, Carmarthen wrote: "No pains . . . shall be spared to cultivate that harmony and good understanding between our two courts, which seems so happily restored by the revolution in the Danish government."[16] Elliot had secured for an isolated Britain a new toehold in Europe.

By 1783, the alliance between Russia and Austria, begun when Catherine and Joseph II met at Mogilyev in 1780, was well known in diplomatic circles.[17] Now Prussia, like Britain, was isolated, the Russian ally having deserted Prussia for Austria. The opportunity for both powers to escape from isolation was provided by Joseph II, who provoked a conflict with the Dutch over navigation of the Scheldt River. In November of 1784, the Austro-Dutch dispute ap-

14. Countess of Minto, *A Memoir of the Right Honorable Hugh Elliot* (Edinburgh, 1868), 150–51, 160, 163, 182–83, 243, 287–295.

15. Elliot to Carmarthen, April 24, 1784; printed in ibid., 294.

16. Carmarthen to Hugh Elliot: June 11, 1784, and June 25, 1784; in *Diplomatic Instructions*, Denmark, 3:208–9.

17. Madariaga, *Armed Neutrality*, 439; Karl A. Roider, *Austria's Eastern Question: 1700–1790* (Princeton, 1982),162.

proached the brink of war. Frederick began to organize the princes of Germany into a league to resist what he called a violation by Austria of the liberties of the German princes. Among the first to join this *Furstenbund* were three German electors, among whom was Britain's George III, who was also the elector of Hanover. The adherence to the *Furstenbund* further cooled Britain's relations with Russia,[18] but it was one more British postwar connection in the Baltic and on the Continent. Unfortunately, France's relations with *her* Baltic ally, Sweden, were less promising.

Gustavus III of Sweden often reminded Louis XVI that Sweden was France's most useful ally in the Baltic Sea. Sweden, like the Ottoman Empire, was a perfect counter weight to the "enormous colossus," Russia.[19] But some observers of French foreign affairs questioned the value of the Swedish alliance and wondered if it was enough. "People are forever saying," the diplomatic observer Favier wrote in 1773, "that we need an ally in the North. They are right. But we need two [allies] there so they can sustain each other and balance the enormous power of Russia in the Baltic."[20] Denmark or Prussia had to be added to the equation. But in 1784, Denmark and Prussia were moving closer to Britain.

Nevertheless, Versailles had long nourished the empty hope that Gustavus would find a way to collaborate with Denmark. A Swedish-Danish alliance, backed by France, would be a formidable counterbalance to Russian power.[21] French diplomats looked back with nostalgia to the powerful alliance system developed between 1725 and 1727, when France, with Britain, Prussia, Sweden, and

18. Ibid., 457.

19. A. Geffroy, *Gustave III et la cour de France* (Paris, 1867), 2:43–44.

20. Favier, "Conjectures raisonnées," 206.

21. Ibid., 221; also, LaHouze to Montmorin, 30 October 1787, Archives des affaires étrangères-correspondance politique-Dannemark (hereafter AAE-cp-Dannemark), 166:113.

Denmark, collaborated to provide a short and rare period of safety against Russian expansion in the Baltic.[22]

In the early 1780s, policymakers at Versailles were troubled by the personality of the Swedish king. Gustavius III's grandiose ambitions, unbridled dissipations, and extravagant expenditures (the latter of which always created demands for more subsidies from France) raised well-founded doubts about his reliability.[23] Aware that his behavior provoked distrust, Gustavus again and again resolved to reform his behavior and do better. But French diplomats in Stockholm were never convinced that his resolutions had any staying power.[24]

Behind French hesitations about Gustavus was the fear that his diplomatic and military ambitions would involve France in international wars not of France's choosing, wars that France could ill afford. In 1780, for example, Gustavus developed a project for a war with Denmark. It included, of course, the assumption that France would assist him. He even planned to visit Paris to discuss his "secret." Realizing that the "secret" was not a secret in the capitals of Europe, Louis XVI advised Gustavus not to include Versailles on his European itinerary.[25]

But it was a Swedish war with Russia that Versailles feared most. Since 1756 France had been part of an alliance system that included Russia. And in 1787 France would complete a commercial treaty with Catherine II, which was partially motivated by the hope that France could influence St. Petersburg through closer commercial ties. While this new approach to Russia was not yet firm or proven, it most certainly would not work if France did not restrain its Swedish ally in the Baltic.

Louis XVI could not abandon Gustavus III, for Sweden's value

22. A. Geffroy, ed., *Recueil des Instructions données aux ambassadeurs et ministres de France* (Paris, 1885), Suède, xc–xci.

23. Ibid., ci.

24. Pons to Vergennes, 1 Oct. 1784, AAE-cp-Suède, 267:259–259vo.

25. A. Geffroy, *Gustave III et la cour de France*, 2:4.

in France's previous European diplomatic strategies was undeniable. So when Gustavus III arrived in France in the summer of 1784, ostensibly to renew his commercial relations with France, he was received with mixed feelings. Louis XVI sincerely wanted to maintain the Swedish connection. And he wanted to further develop Franco-Swedish commerce. But what did Gustavus want? Most of all, he wanted money. He wanted money and in amounts the French minister of finance, Calonne, considered as "exorbitant as they were premature."[26] After intense negotiations, the two monarchs reached some significant agreements. In the Provisional Convention of 1784, France promised to continue the navigation and commercial convention they had agreed to in 1741. In addition, Louis promised to give to Gustavus the island of Saint Barthélemy in the Antilles in return for an entrepôt at Göteborg, Sweden, where products coming from France and its American colonies in French ships could freely enter.[27]

But when discussion came around to subsidies, agreement became more difficult. Louis XVI refused to grant Gustavus the enormous subsidies he wanted. After much haggling, they finally agreed that Louis XVI would pay Gustavus III (over and above the subsidy already granted him in an earlier Franco-Swedish Convention) an additional subsidy of six million livres during the next five years. Gustavus was not at all satisfied with the amount, but Louis reminded him that France had its own considerable debts from the American War and could not "do all that she would like to do for her allies."[28]

In addition, the two monarchs "secretly and privately" agreed

26. AAE-cp-Suède, 276:170.

27. "Provisional Convention for the Explanation of the Preliminary Treaty of Commerce and Navigation of 25 April, 1741 between France and Sweden signed at Versailles, 1 July, 1784," printed in Clive Parry, ed., *Consolidated Treaty Series* (Dobbs Ferry, N.Y., 1969), 49:91–97.

28. A. Geffroy, *Gustave III et la cour de France*, 2:44–45; AAE-cp-Suède, 276:170–171vo.

that if Sweden were attacked in Europe, France would furnish Sweden with 12,000 infantry, a suitable artillery, and a naval squadron composed of twelve ships of the line and six frigates. On the other hand, if France were attacked by sea, Gustavus III promised to provide France with a squadron of eight ships of the line and four frigates. If Britain should intervene in such a way as to make it impossible for either power to meet its military commitments to the other, arrangements were made to translate the military aid into monetary payments.[29]

The new Franco-Swedish agreement did not restore France's fragile confidence in Gustavus III or Sweden. Sweden faced a political crisis similar, ironically, to the one soon to appear in France. Critically weakened by financial and administrative disorder, Sweden saw a swelling discontent among all social classes, especially the nobility, whose power Gustavus had severely reduced in a coup in 1772. Louis XVI's secretary of state for foreign affairs, the comte de Vergennes, who had been France's ambassador to Stockholm in 1772 and one of Gustavus's sources of support during the coup, felt obliged to remind Gustavus that the "essential aim of the Swedish king ought to be to reestablish the population and increase the riches of his state."[30] In his 1783 instructions to the marquis de Pons, Louis XVI's ambassador to Stockholm, Vergennes told the ambassador to try to convince Gustavus of Sweden's need for a "wise economy." What Sweden needed was "peace outside and economy inside."[31] The level of discontent in Sweden was so high, Vergennes feared, there was a real possibility that Swedes opposing Gustavus would seek outside help from a foreign power.[32] That foreign power would certainly be Russia.

29. "Pacte secrète d'amitié et d'union entre le Roi très chrétien et le Roi de Suède fait à Versailles le 19 juillet, 1784," AAE-md-France, 1897:125–176vo.

30. Ibid., 62; A. Geffroy, *Receuil des instructions*, ci.

31. "Mémoire pour servir d'instruction au Marquis de Pons," 4 June 1787, AAE-cp-Suède, Supplement 13:94–94vo.

32. A. Geffroy, *Gustave III et la cour de France*, 2:64–65. As early as 1773, Favier

Gustavus's international ambitions continued to cause anxiety at Versailles. When Gustavus III made his request to Louis XVI for subsidies, he did so with the argument that, if he had the means to augment his armed forces, he could create a "diversion" that France would find "very interesting." The diversion Gustavus III had in mind was a war against Russia. The suggestion energized the opinion already alive at Versailles that Gustavus plotted a military adventure.[33] Louis XVI did not want to find himself obliged to help (or even refuse help to) an old ally.

Thus, when Gustavus left Paris to return to Stockholm, Louis XVI wrote him a personal letter wishing him well in his plans to build up his army and navy. But he ended the letter with the admonition: "Knowing the prudence and wisdom of Your Majesty, I am confident that [you will be] content to provide for the security of your estates, [and] will avoid all demonstrations which could be the subject or even the pretext for anxiety on the part of anyone."[34] But Gustavus's ambitions, his intense passion for glory, and his nagging domestic problems made a foreign war an attractive diversion. An attack on Russia would be especially hard to resist if Russia became involved in another war with the Ottoman Empire.

---

expressed concern that unless Gustavus was able to solve Sweden's domestic political and economic problems, which divided and tore Sweden apart internally, it would be extremely vulnerable to outside intervention. And France, "far away, without any communications with her by land," would be unable to provide much help. See Favier, "Conjectures raissonées . . . ," 215.

33. Note: Calonne to Louis XVI, AAE-cp-Suède, 276:170.

34. Louis XVI to Gustavus III, September 27, 1784, printed in A. Geffroy, *Gustave III et la cour de France*, 2:49–50.

FOUR

The Eastern Question:
The Ottoman Empire

THE UNCERTAIN character of France's northern ally, Sweden, was matched by the steady disintegration of the Ottoman Empire in the south. Louis XVI had no formal treaty of alliance with the Ottoman Empire. Nevertheless, the Turks, as traditional friends of France, played an essential role in French international trade and international politics. From as early as the sixteenth century, French resident merchants had been leaders among Europeans in the Ottoman Empire in organizing trade between the Empire and Europe by means of special "capitulations."[1] An estimated three-fifths of the total of European trade with the Ottoman Empire was in the hands of the French.[2] By the end of the eighteenth century, perhaps as many as two million Frenchmen enjoyed the benefits of the Franco-Ottoman trade.

For years the Ottoman Empire played a central role in France's diplomacy in Eastern Europe and the eastern Mediterranean. Generations of French diplomats saw the Turks as a major chess piece

1. See "Treaty of Amity and Commerce: The Ottoman Empire and France, February, 1535," in J. C. Hurewitz, *Diplomacy in the Near and Middle East* (Princeton, 1956), 1–5.

2. William Hale and Ali Ihsan Bagis, eds., *Four Centuries of Turco-British Relations* (North Yorkshire, 1984), 41.

in Eastern Europe. If Russia or Austria threatened the European balance of power, France counted on the Turks to check them. This was France's classical "Turkish diversion."[3] Because Persia was not perceived at Versailles as a part of Europe's balance of power system, French statesmen discouraged the Turks from spending themselves in wars with their bitter enemies the Persians, in order to ensure that the Turks were readily available when needed in Europe.[4] But the decay of Ottoman power in the eighteenth century called into question the value of the "Turkish diversion."

How should Louis XVI respond to the collapse of the Turks?

Answers to the question circulated freely in the *cabinets* of Versailles. Money, according to one opinion, was "the golden key which opens all locks." If France sent more money for selective distribution in Constantinople, the opinion held, the sultan and his ministers would continue to serve the interests of France. But Louis XVI's secretary of state, Vergennes, knew from thirteen years' personal experience as France's representative to the Ottoman Empire that money had only limited influence at Constantinople.[5]

Others held the opinion that war would solve the problem of Turkish decline. In some mystical way, war would regenerate the Turks. But when Louis XV's minister, Choiseul, succeeded in getting the Turks to war with Russia (1768–74), his success nearly turned into a catastrophe. The Turkish military was simply not up to the task. When the Russians later moved, with Austria's reluctant acquiescence, to annex the Crimea, the Turkish war machine again could do little to stop them. France's frustrations were com-

3. Stanford Shaw, *History of the Ottoman Empire and Modern Turkey* (Cambridge, 1976) 1:255–56; L. P. Ségur, *Politique de tous les cabinets de l'Europe* (Paris, 1801), 1:359–60, 365–66; 3:114–15; Archives des affaires étrangères—correspondance politique-Turquie (hereafter referred to as AAE-cp-Turquie), 128:20–20vo.

4. AAE-cp-Turquie, 128:19–19vo.

5. Vergennes to Rouillé, 17 Aug. 1755, in ibid., 129:69–71; Vergennes to Choiseul, 28 May, 1766, in ibid., 142:96–96vo; Saint-Priest, *Mémoires sur l'ambassade de France en Turquie* (Paris, 1877), 150–55.

pounded.[6] Both the maréchal de Castries and the maréchal de Ségur, Louis XVI's secretaries of state for the navy and army respectively, argued that France should attack Austria or its possessions in order to halt the further spoliation of the Ottoman Empire.[7] But Louis XVI rejected that option. Joseph II was his brother-in-law, and France needed the Austrian alliance as long as Great Britain remained hostile.

Part of the difficulty Louis XVI had in dealing with the Ottoman Empire could be traced to legacies of the past. In the First Treaty of Versailles, signed in May of 1756, France ceased its longstanding hostility to Austria and agreed to a defensive alliance.[8] Later, in January of the next year, Russia joined the French and the Austrians in the Second Treaty of Versailles.[9] Since war against the Porte was not specifically excluded from the articles requiring France to assist its new allies, the Turks understandably felt they had been abandoned by France and left to the mercy of their enemies.[10] The French treaties with Austria (there was a Third Treaty

6. The Austrian response to the Russian annexation of the Crimea is described in Karl Roider, *Austria's Eastern Question: 1700–1790* (Princeton, 1982), 165–68.

7. M. S. Anderson,"The Great Powers and the Russian Annexation of the Crimea, 1783–84," *Slavonic and East European Review* 37 (1958–59): 32.

8. "Convention de neutralité entre S. M. Chrétienne et S. M. l'Imp. Reine de Hongrie et de Bohême signé à Versailles, 1 May 1756," Frederick August W. Wenck, *Codex juris gentium recentissimi* (Leipzig, 1781–95), 3:139–41; "Traité d'amitié et d'alliance," ibid., 3:141–47; "Cinq articles séparés," in Christophe G. Koch, *Recueil des Traités et actes diplomatiques* (Basle, 1802), 2:11–16.

9. Rouillé to Vergennes, 1 June 1756, AAE-cp-Turquie, 132:56–61; L. Jay Olivia, *Misalliance: A Study of French Policy in Russia during the Seven Years' War* (New York, 1964), 34–36, 44–45; "Acte d'accession de la Russie au traité de Versailles du 1 mai, 1756," in Georg G. Martens, *Supplément au Recueil des principaux traités* (Gottingue, 1807), 3:33–36; see also Fedor F. Martens, *Recueil des traités et conventions conclu par la Russie avec les puissances étrangères* (St. Petersburg, 1874–1909), 9:352ff.; "Traité d'union et d'amitié défensif entre la France et l'Autriche," Christophe G. Koch, *Recueil des traités et actes diplomatiques*, 2:43–81.

10. L. P. Ségur, *Politique de tous les cabinets . . .*, 1:370ff.; Vergennes to Rouille, 22 July, 18 August 1756, AAE-cp-Turquie, 32:158–159, 202–12; "Notes tiré des anec-

of Versailles concluded in March of 1759) and indirect ties with Russia created lasting suspicions of France at Constantinople.[11] Consequently, this so-called "Diplomatic Revolution" of 1756 began a slow but dangerous erosion of France's traditional ties with the Porte.

Long-term economic developments also undermined France's historical relations with the Ottoman Empire. Neither French diplomats nor French merchants ever saw that their commercial relations with the Ottoman Empire contributed to the very instability that made the Turks an increasingly uncertain friend. Traditionally, a huge artisan class had been the keystone of the economic structure and prosperity of the empire. But their security was undermined by the intrusion of Western goods, especially French textiles manufactured by more modern techniques. The result was urban unemployment and unrest.[12]

Moreover, the growing European demand for grain created in the provinces of the Ottoman Empire a flourishing, but for the most part illegal, international grain trade and fostered the rise of a class, the *ayan*, who acquired and consolidated estates in response to the West's demand for grain. The transformation to market-oriented production meant a ruthless exploitation of the rural population. Tradition held that the sultan was personally responsible for the welfare of his subjects, but the rise of the *ayan* meant a diminishing of the sultan's ability to control the supply and price of grain, since the *ayan* were powerful enough to ignore or resist his authority. When the cost of grain increased beyond the means of the poor, the sultan was unable to do anything about

---

dotes du chavalier Porter," in ibid., 90–91; Rouillé to Vergennes, 27 June 1756, in ibid., 83–84vo; Comte de Saint Priest, *Mémoires sur l'ambassade de France en Turquie* (Paris, 1877), 152–53; L. Jay Oliva, *Misalliance*, 46–69.

11. Favier, "Conjectures raissonnées . . ." in Ségur, *Politique de tous les cabinets*, 2:12–13.

12. Deena R. Sadat, "Rumeli Ayanlari: The Eighteenth Century," *Journal of Modern History* 44, no. 3 (1972), 355.

it.[13] His ineffectiveness as the "father of his subjects" had a crippling effect on his authority.

Nothing shocked Frenchmen in the Ottoman Empire more than the brutality sometimes occasioned by the sultan's exercise of power.[14] But the perception many Frenchmen had of Turkish despotism was a misleading caricature.[15] In fact, the perception was often contradicted by the experiences alert French diplomats had in the empire. In their correspondence and memoirs they repeatedly described situations in which the sultan was not all-powerful and occasions when he endured severe restraints on his authority. Turkish officials bargained with the sultan over budgets and sometimes even refused to obey him.[16] The sultan could never touch the property of the Ulema, the religious "learned men" in charge of interpreting and enforcing Islamic law.[17] The sultan was obliged by tradition to appear in the mosque every Friday to be seen by the public; otherwise, there was a public tumult.[18] French diplomats seemed to understand that any act of the sultan (or any of his officials) that violated the *Qur'an* was illegal.[19] In reality the sultan's power was limited and unsure. But the French government

13. For a more detailed discussion of the consequences of the Ottoman Empire's economic relations with the West, see ibid., esp. 348–55.

14. Hamilton Gibb and Harold Bowen, *Islamic Society and the West* (New York, 1950), 1:120–21.

15. David Young, "Montesquieu's View of Despotism and His Use of Travel Literature," *Review of Politics* 40 (1978): 392–405.

16. Baron de Tott, *Mémoires sur les Turcs et les Tarters* (Amsterdam, 1784), Pt. III, 11; René Moreux, "La situation de la France dans le Levant à la fin du XVIIIe siècle," *Revue d'histoire moderne et contemporaine* 3 (1901–3): 617–18.

17. Baron de Tott, *Mémoires*, Pt. I, 27.

18. Ibid., Pt. I, 100–111.

19. Saint-Priest, "Mémoire sur le commerce et la navigation de la France en Levant," printed in Charles Schefer, ed., Saint Priest, *Mémoires sur l'ambassade de France en Turquie*, 316; Charles Gravier, Comte de Vergennes, "Mémoire sur la Porte Ottoman," in L. P. Ségur, *Politique de tous les cabinets de l'Europe . . .*, 3:143–44.

at Versailles and those who represented it abroad continued to see the sultan as a "despot." The stereotype clouded their vision.[20] An erosion of the sultan's power was especially noticeable as one approached the outer frontiers of the empire. The sultan was the nominal head of the Ottoman Empire, but some provinces hardly recognized his authority. Egypt, for example, was all but independent. In Armenia, the political ties to the sultan barely existed. Reports of unrest and revolts against the sultan were frequent in the correspondence of diplomats.[21] The Russians repeatedly complained that, because the sultan was losing his grip on the empire, the Turks no longer policed their own populations. Russia (according to the Russians) therefore had to maintain expensive armies along its Ottoman frontiers to keep brigands and Tartars from crossing the borders and raiding Russian subjects and territories.[22]

Thus, two ingredients compounded the crisis facing the Ottoman Empire during the last decades of the eighteenth century: the disintegration of a traditional empire that had long enjoyed the trappings and reality of power and the aggressive, expanding character of a Europe armed with a military, commercial, and manufacturing technology as yet foreign to the Turks.[23] In addition, wars

20. Montesquieu, also, never quite reconciled his political definition of despotism with all the information provided him by the literature of travelers, diplomats, and merchants knowledgeable about the Near East. See David Young, "Montesquieu's View of Despotism . . . ," 401–5; also, Sven Stelling-Michaud, "Le mythe du despotisme oriental," *Schweizer Beitrage zur Allgemeinen Geschichte* 18–19 (1960–61): 328–40.

21. William Eton, *A Survey of the Turkish Empire* (London, 1809), 275–84; on reports and predictions of revolts and unrest see, for example, Vergennes to Choiseul-Gouffier, 11 Jan. 1787; Choiseul-Gouffier to Vergennes, 11 Jan. 1787; Choiseul-Gouffier to Montmorin, 3 Aug. 1787; AAE-cp-Turquie, 175:10, 14–14vo; 176:69–78vo.

22. Choiseul-Gouffier to Vergennes, 25 Jan. 1787, in ibid., 175:48vo; Belland to Montmorin, 17 May 1787, AAE-cp-Russie, 121:22–29vo.

23. Stanford Shaw, *History of the Ottoman Empire and Modern Turkey*, 1:217–76; William Eton, *A Survey of the Turkish Empire*, 231–33.

had drained the tremendous strength of the Turks, and inflation plagued the economy. High taxes crippled both agriculture and trade. Frequent food shortages and high prices led to famine and malnutrition, which in turn made the population vulnerable to disease and plague.[24] The loss of territories and international preeminence eroded Ottoman influence and morale. Military defeat fueled domestic conflict.

Reforms were attempted, but the basic issue was always whether reform could be undertaken within the framework of traditional Ottoman culture.[25] Conservatives believed that Ottoman decline came from the failure to adhere to the old ideas, practices, and religious traditions, which centuries earlier had accompanied Ottoman success and magnificence. In contrast, others wanted to open Ottoman society and culture to the West, to learn to use and develop Western military technology, to create with the printing press an "enlightenment" that included Western ideas, science, and methods of scholarship.[26] They hoped to borrow Western techniques of manufacturing to respond to the economic collapse of traditional Ottoman craft industries and meet the competition of Western, especially French, imports manufactured by newer technologies.[27] The Grand Vizir Huseyin Pasha, for example, did his best to encourage manufacturing processes that could compete with the Europeans. The comte de Bonneval and the baron de Tott, both Western military advisers, were brought in by reforming sultans to modernize the Turkish military and try to raise it to the technical and organizational level of European militaries.[28]

But reforms introduced by pro-Westerners created a deep schism in Ottoman society. Traditionalists clung to the older ways because they sincerely felt they were superior. They received almost unanimous support from Islamic religious leaders. Western ideas

24. Baron de Tott, *Mémoires*, Pt. I, 38–40; Pt. II, 146; Pt. III, 28.
25. Stanford Shaw, *History of the Ottoman Empire and Modern Turkey*, 1:175.
26. Ibid., 1:234–38, 265–66.   27. Ibid., 1:225.
28. Ibid., 1:240–42, 250–52, 257.

consequently brought to the Ottoman Empire fierce ideological, religious, and cultural conflicts, which Western diplomats, including the French, did not thoroughly understand. At the same time, the failures of the empire in the international arena brought a growing dependence on Western powers, especially France, for diplomatic and military support. France found itself, therefore, at the center of a dangerous storm within the Ottoman Empire.[29] Hindered by inadequate communications (for Constantinople was the most distant of all the French embassies)[30] and confounded by distorted stereotypes about the powers of the sultan, French statesmen in the last decades of the eighteenth century watched Russia absorb more and more Turkish territory, while Austria maneuvered to gain whatever spoils it could snatch from Turkish weakness.

No one in France saw that Turkish problems were a microcosm of a larger pattern of European and Mediterranean changes just appearing on the horizon. Both the Ottoman Empire and Europe were beginning to experience the economic dislocations caused when skilled artisans were faced with the competition of new manufacturing technology. Both regions saw the development of a capitalist agriculture, which sold where profits were high and not necessarily where hunger was rampant. Like France, the Ottoman Empire felt the ever-more-serious fiscal crises of governments caught in the whirlpools of war. Both France and the Turks saw their rulers increasingly unable to reform, because of the resistance of powerful and privileged interests. Unfortunately, Turkish understanding of the West was as rigidly limited as Western understanding of the Turks. The ignorance and contempt of some Turks for the West, their blinders of fanaticism, pride, and arrogance regarding their superiority, kept them from comprehending most

29. Ibid., 1:255–56.

30. Pierre du Parc, ed., *Recueil des Instructions aux ambassadeurs et ministres de France . . .*(Paris, 1969), 29 Turquie, xxxvi.

of the implications of their relations with Westerners.[31] Thus, as the eighteenth century drew to a close, the Turks grappled with a fundamental crisis in their society, and neither Frenchmen nor Turks fully appreciated the many dimensions of that crisis. Favier wrote in 1773 that the Turks were able to see the Christian powers from only two perspectives: war and commerce.[32] The French perceptions of the Ottoman Empire were mirror images of the same perspectives.

In January of 1787 France signed a commercial treaty with Russia. The treaty was viewed at Versailles as part of a plan to push the British out of their monopoly of trade with Russia. Indeed, the British soon began to feel the effects of the new treaty, because they were unable to renew their own commercial treaty with the Russians. Catherine stubbornly refused to commit herself to any treaty until the British accepted the principles of Russia's armed neutrality, and the British would not agree to that condition. But while statesmen at Versailles enjoyed watching discontent in Britain mount over the success of France in completing a commercial treaty with Russia,[33] they were less pleased when the Turks bluntly asked if the Franco-Russian treaty meant that the sultan could no longer count on French support.[34] At the same time, the British representative in Constantinople energetically schemed to destroy the credibility of the French. He launched a campaign to convince

31. Ibid., xxxii.

32. Favier, "Conjectures raisonnées," 2:24–25.

33. Belland to Vergennes, 19 January 1787, Archives des affaires étrangères-correspondance politique-Russie (hereafter AAE-cp-Russie), 20:40–45. On the negotiations for the Franco-Russian treaty of 1787 there are two excellent articles: J. L. van Regemorter, "Commerce et Politique: préparation et négotiation du traité franco-russe de 1787," *Cahiers du Monde Russe et Sovietique* 4, no. 3. (July-September, 1963), 230–57; Frank Fox, "Negotiating with the Russians: Ambassador Ségur's Mission to Saint Petersburg, 1784–1789," *French Historical Studies* 7, no. 1 (1971), 47–71.

34. Choiseul-Gouffier to Vergennes, 10 Feb. 1787, AAE-cp-Turquie, 175:55–55vo; Montmorin to Ségur, 15 March 1787, AAE-cp-Russie, 120:137–138vo.

the Turks that the Russo-French Commercial Treaty was, in fact, Catherine's reward to Louis XVI for a promise to abandon the sultan.[35]

Despite the unraveling of the Franco-Turkish friendship, Louis XVI wanted to preserve the Ottoman Empire and French influence there. Above all, he hoped to avoid a sudden collapse of the empire which, he believed, would surely bring instability and war to Eastern Europe. His minister, Vergennes, agreed and argued that France's refusal to participate in any partition of the Ottoman Empire would help avoid a sudden death.[36] Louis XVI, therefore, sought the cooperation of European powers such as Britain and Austria to work out a formula to assist the "sick man" of Europe.[37]

Until 1783, France's involvement in the American Revolutionary War absorbed France's energies. As the war closed, however, Louis XVI began to put out feelers to Britain to see if the two powers could collaborate to support the Turks in their failing European position.[38] He was convinced that Great Britain, as well as France, had a vested interest in defending the integrity of the Turks. If

35. Montmorin to Ségur, 22 March 1787, in ibid., 120:166–171vo.

36. 23 June 1785, AAE-cp-Turquie, 69; quoted in Francois Charles-Roux, "La politique française en Egypt à la fin au XVIIIe siècle," *Revue historique* 92 (1906):10–12. See also: Charles Gravier, Comte de Vergennes, "Mémoire au roi, 29 April, 1784," Archives Nationales, K 161; Vergennes's "Mémoire sur la Porte Ottomane," printed in L. P. Ségur, *Politique de tous les les cabinets . . .* , 3:143ff. Also, Ségur's comments on the above "Mémoire," ibid., 3:154; Charles de Chambrun, *A l'école d'un diplomate: Vergennes* (Paris, 1944), 401–12.

37. Without Franco-British cooperation, the Ottoman Empire was increasingly vulnerable to Russian and even Austrian attacks. See M. S. Anderson, "Great Britain and the Russo-Turkish War of 1768–74," *English Historical Review* 69 (1954): 58; M. S. Anderson, "The Great Powers and the Russian Annexation of the Crimea, 1783–84," *Slavonic and East European Review* 37 (1958–59): 20, 22–23, 24–25.

38. "Memoire pour servir d'Instruction au sieur Comte d'Adhémar, . . . allant en Angleterre en qualité d'ambassadeur de la part de Sa Majesté, 25 April, 1783," printed in Paul Vaucher, ed., *Recueil des Instructions aux ambassadeurs et ministres de France . . .* , (Paris, 1965), Angleterre, vol. XXV-2, tome 3, 522.

Russian power continued to grow at the expense of the Turks in the south and the Swedes in the north, both Britain and France would be faced with a formidable maritime power capable of dominating the Baltic Sea and the Eastern Mediterranean.[39] The British conquest of India in the eighteenth century meant that Britain needed access to India. Should a hostile Russia gain control of the Straits of the Bosphorus and the Dardenelles, the shortest British route to India would be endangered.[40]

This common set of interests contained the seed for a Franco-British rapprochement, and Louis XVI tried to cultivate it. One result of France's campaign to find some avenue of understanding with Great Britain was the Anglo-French (or Eden) Commercial Treaty of 1786. Louis XVI hoped to bring together the British and French commercial economies, thereby establishing ties of mutual interest and influence, especially with regard to Eastern Europe. But there were many obstacles in the path to a Franco-British *détente*. In the first place, the British government showed very little concern for the commerce or integrity of the Ottoman Empire during the three decades before the French Revolution. At the moment of the Anglo-French Commercial Treaty of 1786, Pitt was much more interested in developing trade with Russia than with the Levant, where British trading interests languished. In 1779, for example, the British ambassador to Constantinople, Robert Ainsley, had reported to London that not a single English ship had reached Constantinople in the preceding eight months.[41]

Furthermore, the long-standing suspicions and hostilities that separated France and Great Britain could not easily be cleared away. Louis XVI recognized that the task of reconciliation was del-

39. Ibid.

40. William Hale and Ali Ihsan Bagis, eds., *Four Centuries of Turco-British Relations* (North Yorkshire, 1984), 2

41. Ibid., 42–43; see also, Ali Ihsan Bagis, "The Advent of British Interests in the Integrity of the Ottoman Empire," *Hacettepe University Bulletin of Social Science*, no. 1 (Dec. 1978): 102–18.

icate and controversial. In France and Britain powerful individuals were shocked by the suggestion that France and Great Britain could co-exist; they strenuously opposed any cooperation between the two great powers. The British could not easily forget that the defeat of George III in the American War was to a large extent the work of France.[42] Moreover, as it turned out, the difficulties of execution of the Anglo-French Commercial Treaty, the treaty intended to bring France and Great Britain together, only further aggravated relations between the two powers.[43] Nevertheless, as late as 1788 the comte de Montmorin, who replaced Vergennes at Foreign Affairs, still pursued the fading hope of Franco-British cooperation in Eastern Europe. Occasionally he thought he saw signs that the British cabinet was interested in nurturing "good harmony" with France. But neither he nor Louis XVI could ignore the hatred that had separated the two powers for so long.[44] Finally, when the British joined the Prussians in 1787 and intervened against French interests in the Dutch Republic, hopes for an accommodation with Britain all but vanished. The intervention, Montmorin lamented, had "established between the two sovereigns [George III and Louis XVI] a system of distrust which, henceforth, will be difficult, if not impossible, to dispel."[45] There seemed to be no way to break down the wall of hostility that divided Versailles and London.

The Franco-Russian Commercial Treaty of 1787 created ties be-

42. Vaucher, ed., *Recueil des Instructions aux ambassadeurs et ministres de France* . . . , 515, 522–23.

43. Marie Donaghay, "The Best Laid Plans: French Execution of the Anglo-French Commercial Treaty of 1786," *European History Quarterly* 14 (1984): 401–22. And Marie Donaghay, "Textiles and the Anglo-French Commercial Treaty of 1786," *Textile History* 13, no. 2 (1982), 215–20.

44. "Mémoire pour servir d'Instruction au Sieur Chevalier de La Luzerne, . . . allant à Londres pour y resider en qualité de son ambassadeur auprès de Sa Majesté Britannique, 7 January, 1788," in Vaucher, ed., *Recueil des instructions*, 540–41.

45. Ibid., 541.

tween Catherine and Louis XVI that Versailles believed would make it possible to exercise more influence on Russian policy regarding the Ottoman Empire. But France's attempt to mediate Russo-Turkish differences created suspicions both in St. Petersburg and in Constantinople. The Russians suspected that French attempts to mediate simply provided the Turks with time to rearm.[46] The Turks, in turn, questioned the value of French mediation when Louis seemed to be abandoning Constantinople in favor of St. Petersburg.[47] Nevertheless, Versailles continued to provide the Turks with technical assistance and military advisers to help them modernize their military and put their defenses in order.[48] At the same time, Louis again and again explained to Catherine why he could not approve of any attempts on the territory of the Ottoman Empire.[49]

Predictably, French military assistance for the Turks caused alarm in St. Petersburg. Prince Potemkin could not understand why France, considered to be "the most enlightened [nation] in the universe," protected the Turks, who represented "pestilence and barbarism" in the bosom of Europe.[50] But Louis XVI had his own interests to protect. His representative at Constantinople continued to play the mediator as the disagreements between the Turks and the Russians multiplied daily. By February of 1787, however, it seemed only a matter of time before the tensions created by so many disputes exploded into a new Russo-Turkish war.[51] France

46. Belland to Vergennes, n.d. March 1787, AAE-cp-Russie, 120:125–32.

47. "Extrait d'une lettre écrit au Ministre des affaires étrangères par M. le Comte de Choiseul-Gouffier, 25 Jan. 1787," in ibid., 120:52–57vo.

48. Choiseul-Gouffier to Montmorin, 24 March 1787, AAE-cp-Turquie, 175:138–47; Montmorin to Ségur, 15 March 1787, AAE-cp-Russie, 120:139–40; Montmorin to Choiseul-Gouffier, 26 April 1787, AAE-cp-Turquie, 175:230vo.

49. Montmorin to Segur, 15 March 1787, AAE-cp-Russie, 120:140.

50. Segur to Montmorin, 7 April 1787," ibid., 120:224–224vo.

51. Belland to Vergennes, 21 February 1787, ibid., 120:96–106; Choiseul-Gouffier to Montmorin, 24 July 1787, AAE-cp-Turquie, 176:55.

would then face the difficult task of choosing between an old friend and a new ally. Both choices entailed equally unsatisfactory consequences. Meanwhile, at the other end of the European continent, France cautiously explored the possibilities of a new relationship with its old enemy, Great Britain.

PART II

The Effacement of France

The Fatal Anglo-French (Eden)
Commercial Treaty of 1786

IN THE summer of 1785 the French government sent a polite but firm warning to London that the old Commercial Convention of Utrecht, a treaty dating back to 1713, would no longer be the basis of British-French trade. Versailles followed up the warning with a number of decrees restricting foreign trade with France; they hit British merchants with particular force. Vergennes, Louis XVI's secretary of state for foreign affairs, predicted that these measures and their spectacular suddenness would "make some sensation in London."[1]

They did.

Within a few months, British merchants were doing as Versailles had hoped they would do: they were urging their government to negotiate a new commercial treaty with France. Versailles then applied additional pressure by prohibiting the entry into France of British hardwares. At the same time the French government announced incentives to attract foreign manufactures to come to France and establish new manufactures in France, which would compete with those in Britain.

<hr />

1. Quoted in Marie Donaghay, "The Ghosts of Ruined Ships: The Commercial Treaty of 1786 and the Lessons of the Past," *The Proceedings of the Consortium on Revolutionary Europe* (Athens, Ga., 1981), 113.

France's commerce with Britain during the eighteenth century was governed by the Commercial Convention of Utrecht of 1713. But it was a flawed instrument. Since the mid-seventeenth century, British-French commerce had been subject to numerous prohibitions and high tariffs. High duties on the products of each country entering the realm of the other were, in theory, protective walls to shield producers of each country from the competition of imports. In 1701, for example, Louis XIV issued a decree forbidding the entry into France of most manufactured goods from England, and he placed exorbitant duties on most other English products. Britain raised import duties on French goods by an average of 400 percent from 1690 to 1704 and prohibited import of all French products during the wars of the League of Augsburg and Spanish Succession. By the eighteenth century, Britain's import duties on French imports ranged from fifty to seventy-five percent of value.

During the peace negotiations of 1713, the French and the English in articles eight and nine of the Commercial Convention of Utrecht (1713) stipulated that their trade would be on the basis of the most favored nation. They also eliminated all prohibitions on products from both countries and lowered to the levels of 1664 (with some exceptions) duties on products coming from either country to the other. But when the bill to approve the critical articles eight and nine came before the British Parliament, it was rejected.

Nevertheless, the British government continued to pursue a trade agreement with France, even promising the two French representatives in London that a better commercial treaty between France and Britain would surely be approved by the next Parliament after the soon-to-be-held elections. But a better commercial treaty turned out to be much more difficult than anyone imagined. Unfortunately, British and French merchants were unfamiliar with each other's business practices. And before they could even initiate a serious consideration of trade and customs duties, they had to discover what products each country produced and which they wanted to trade. Negotiations continued, but endless talks, proposals, and counter-proposals brought fatigue and frayed tempers. In September of 1714 the French representatives in London went home with the promise that they would soon return to renew discussions. But they never came back. And the gutted Commercial Convention of Utrecht remained the basis of British-French trade. It maintained many of the old regulations, but some of them were never enforced.[2] Most legal commerce was now prohibited or prohibitively costly. By the late eighteenth century, the greater part of the trade between France and Britain was in the hands of smugglers. Probably three-quarters of what was imported into France was contraband.[3] A better trade relationship between France and Britain had to wait until after the War of the American Revolution.

Despite sustained British resistance, the peace treaty of 1783 between France and Britain contained, in article eighteen, the promise that after the two parties exchanged ratifications of the treaty, they would name commissioners to prepare new commercial arrangements between the two nations. These arrangements would be based on "reciprocity and mutual convenience." The article further mandated that the commissioners should finish their task within two years. In a Counter-Declaration in the same treaty, the king of France explained that the purpose of the new negotiations was not to destroy any privileges, advantages, or regulations

2. My summary of these negotiations in 1713–14 for an Anglo-French commercial treaty owes much to Thomas J. Schaeper, "French and English Trade after the Treaty of Utrecht: The Missions of Anisson and Fénellon in London, 1713–1714," *British Journal for Eighteenth Century Studies* 9 (1986): 1–18, and Marie Donaghay, "The Ghosts of Ruined Ships," 111–18. Schaeper musters evidence to indicate that the British government actually engineered the defeat of the Parliamentary bill to approve in order to return and negotiate another treaty that would gain more favorable concessions from the French. Certainly this is what the French government suspected.

3. Reginald E. Rabb, *The Role of William Eden in William Pitt's Liberal Trade Policy* (New York, 1942), 36.

contained in the 1713 treaty, but to remedy their defects. His Majesty Louis XVI hoped, therefore, that the project would be pursued with the same good faith and spirit of conciliation that had conditioned the treaty of peace.[4]

This Anglo-French Commercial Treaty resulted from a multitude of French motives. In a memoir read before the Council of State in 1786, the first secretary of the Ministry of Foreign Affairs, Gérard de Raynaval, stressed the advantages to France that might follow from better British-French commercial relations. The wealth of France, Raynaval believed, flowed from its productive agriculture. Increased export trade would stimulate French agriculture by opening foreign markets to French wines which, in 1786, glutted the market.[5] On the other hand, Rayneval said, Britain had flourishing hardware and cotton manufacturers who could sell their goods in France. But there were also French manufactured products such as plate glass, linens, silks, and porcelain that could benefit from expanded trade with Britain.[6] Thus, a trade agreement between the two nations would allow each to trade what it best produced and both would benefit. Products such as textiles, which both countries manufactured, posed more difficult problems that demanded special and reciprocal arrangements.

The French government was fully aware that a significant sector of French manufacturing would object to opening the borders to British manufactured goods. Objections would be especially strong in those sectors where French technology lagged behind that of

4. "Definitive Treaty of Peace and Friendship between France and Great Britain, signed at Versailles, 3 September 1783," in Clive Parry, ed., *The Consolidated Treaty Series* (Dobbs Ferry, N.Y., 1969), 48:437–58.

5. Marie Donaghay, "The Exchange of Products of the Soil and Industrial Goods in the Anglo-French Commercial Treaty of 1786," *Journal of European Economic History* 19 (Fall 1990): 379–83; Oscar Browning, *The Treaty of Commerce between England and France in 1786*, vol. 2, n.s., Transactions of the Royal Historical Society (London, 1885), 357–69.

6. Donaghay, "The Exchange of Products of the Soil," 400.

Britain. Some French manufacturers, consequently, would feel the pinch and pain from British competition. But the competition itself, Rayneval predicted in his report to the council, would have a long-term beneficial effect, since it would compel French manufacturers to upgrade their technology and refine their processes. A trade treaty with Britain, therefore, could be an instrument to accelerate modernization.[7]

Vergennes, the secretary of state for foreign affairs, put forth other reasons for a commercial treaty with Britain. He saw improved trade relations as a way of linking the economic interests of France and Britain. Once the two economies were meshed, France might have greater leverage to influence decisions made in London. British foreign-policy interests, Vergennes was convinced, always gave way to British commercial interests.[8] If France and Britain traded with each other they might, over time, learn to cooperate in diplomatic affairs. A British-French combination would carry considerable weight in Europe. Vergennes suggested that if Britain and France worked together they could find a way to stop Russian expansion in Eastern Europe and help ensure the peace of Europe.[9] When William Eden arrived in France early in 1786 to begin discussions on a commercial treaty, he was immediately introduced to the idea that "England and France ought to unite in some solemn plan of permanent peace."[10]

7. Wilma Pugh, "Calonne's 'New Deal,'" *Journal of Modern History* 11 (1939): 301; Oscar Browning, *The Treaty of Commerce between England and France*, 356–60.

8. "Considérations sur la possibilité d'une alliance entre la France et l'Angleterre, 1774," AAE-md-Angleterre, 56:115–16; Léon Cahen, "Une nouvelle interprétation du traité Franco-Anglais de 1786–1787," *Revue historique* 185 (January-June, 1939): 258; Marie Donaghay provides a summary discussion of Vergennes's motives for an Anglo-French commercial treaty in her unpublished paper "Vergennes and the Anglo-French Commercial Treaty of 1786," delivered at the annual meeting of the Society for French Historical Studies, Columbia, S.C., 1988.

9. Cahen, "Une nouvelle interprétation," 267.

10. Eden to Carmarthen, 17 April, 6 June 1786, in William Eden, "Letters and papers from Mr. Eden relative to the negotiation of the Anglo-French Commer-

Another motive for the commercial treaty found its most articulate spokesman in Dupont de Nemours, who was an inspector-general of commerce. Dupont's reputation as an expert on economic affairs made him a powerful advocate for the treaty. The idea of legitimizing contraband by lowering duties to the level where it was cheaper to trade legally than illegally suggested a way of increasing customs revenues.[11] Dupont argued that if France and England significantly lowered customs duties on goods moving back and forth across the Channel, customs revenues would rise, because smuggling, which everyone agreed was widespread, would become unprofitable. The idea of increased customs revenues was attractive to officials in the French treasury who, by 1786, were struggling to keep afloat in the turbulence of the postwar financial crisis.[12]

But Britain was in no hurry to name commissioners to negotiate a new commercial treaty. They hoped, apparently, to let the matter die from neglect. And when they were finally persuaded to send a commissioner, he arrived in Versailles with no powers to negotiate. But Louis XVI did not plan to let article eighteen disappear into the archives. He determined that the Commercial Convention of Utrecht would be either enforced or replaced.[13] Ver-

---

cial Treaty of 1786 to the British secretary of state," 21–22. The originals of the letters are in *Public Records Office*, London, State Papers, Foreign Office, France. I consulted the microfilm copies collected by the historical library of the Hagley Museum, Wilmington, Delaware. Hereafter referred to as the Eden Papers.

11. Dupont de Nemours's official argument for lowering customs duties to raise revenue is found in "Réflexions sur le bien que peuvent se faire réciproquement la France et l'Angleterre," AAE-md-Angleterre, 65:3–8; see also J. Holland Rose, *William Pitt and National Revival* (London, 1911), 344.

12. Dupont's role in the Anglo-French Commercial Treaty is described in Orville T. Murphy, "Dupont de Nemours and the Anglo-French Commercial Treaty of 1786," *Economic History Review* 19, no. 3 (1966), 569–80.

13. Oscar Browning, *The Treaty of Commerce between England and France*, 357–60; Marie Donaghay, "Textiles and the Anglo-French Commercial Treaty of 1786," *Textile History* 13, no. 2 (1982), 205; Léon Cahen, "Une nouvelle interprétation," 258–60.

gennes knew the British were lukewarm about negotiating a commercial treaty with France, so he looked for a way to provoke them to live up to their end of the agreement as recorded in article eighteen of the 1783 peace treaty—thus the sudden and dramatic restrictive measures of the summer of 1785 described above. By November, the harassing decrees brought the desired result: Pitt decided it was time to negotiate a commercial treaty with France. The message French statesmen read in the British decision to confer was the one they had already predicted: trade, indeed, was a very effective weapon for changing British diplomatic behavior.[14] By September of 1786 France and Britain had signed a commercial treaty and the following January they met to clarify in an additional convention certain unresolved points.[15]

The Anglo-French Commercial Treaty of 1786 did not establish free trade between the two parties. It established "a reciprocal and entirely perfect liberty of navigation and commerce between the subjects" of England and France by establishing guidelines for the protection of the subjects and merchants of both sovereigns and defining principles to govern relations between the two states. While the treaty did not establish free trade, its signing could have opened the way to easing tensions between the two hostile powers.

Individual subjects of the two monarchies were given special assurances and benefits by the treaty to assure their safety. If Britain and France were to "interrupt their friendship" or go to war with each other, subjects of either monarch visiting or living in the realm of the other would not be troubled in any manner if they obeyed the laws. But if their actions were suspect and they were asked to leave, expatriates would be given one year to settle their affairs before departure.

Each of the two signing parties also promised to see to it that the subjects of either country would not commit "acts of hostility"

14. "Considérations sur la possibilité d'une alliance entre la France et l'Angleterre, 1774," AAE-md-Angleterre, 56:121.

15. Clive Parry, ed., *Consolidated Treaty Series* (Dobbs Ferry, N.Y., 1969), 50:139.

or violence against the other on land as well as on the seas. Furthermore, neither government would issue commissions or letters of "repraisals" that would permit individuals to arm vessels and engage in privateering against the ships and cargos of the other. They also agreed that subjects and inhabitants of their respective states could freely and safely enter and leave the territories of either without special permission or safe conduct. Individuals could buy and sell anything necessary for their subsistence or usage, if they did not break the law and provided that they lived peaceably. Finally, the subjects of the two Majesties were free to transport and carry on their commerce in the "land, states, cities, ports, places and rivers" of both sovereigns. They could stay as long as they wished, store in warehouses or depots the merchandise brought from elsewhere, and sell it without restrictions. Thus, an important aim of the treaty was to reduce frictions that might arise among subjects of Britain and France by creating an easy, safe, and secure exchange of persons and goods between the two. Possible future disagreements between France and Britain over definitions of contraband were addressed by articles that narrowly defined contraband to include only arms, ammunition, belts, helmets, horses, and harnesses.

The treaty represented a partial victory for the overstocked French wines. England agreed not to charge higher custom duties on French wines than were then paid on wines from Portugal. But Britain reserved the right to lower rates on Portuguese wines at some later date. French vinegar benefitted from a reduction of duties by more than one-half. French *eaux-de-vie* duties received a modest cut of almost two shillings a gallon. Duties on olive oils from France were set at the level of the most favored nation. Duties on gauzes, hardware, cutlery, cabinet ware, or turnery and goods of iron, steel, copper, or brass could not be more than ten percent *ad valorem*. The two parties agreed on a fixed duty of twelve percent on cottons, woolens, millinery made of muslim, linen, cambric, or gauze, on porcelain, plate-glass, pottery, mirrors, and crystal. Shippers of saddlery would pay a fifteen percent *ad valorem* customs duty. A hefty duty of thirty percent was charged for beer. But textiles of cotton and wool mixed with silk were prohibited altogether. All other goods not mentioned in the treaty were to be taxed at whatever rate the most favored nation enjoyed.

A month after the signatures were placed on the additional convention, Vergennes was dead. The procedural negotiations and the reforms necessary to the smooth operation of the new trade agreement were now left to new ministers, to the secretary of state for foreign affairs, Montmorin, and to ministers such as Calonne (replaced in April 1787 by Fourqueux), Brienne, and Castries who, despite their efforts, were handicapped by their lack of experience or a limited understanding of what they needed to do to make the new treaty work.[16] Their effectiveness was also impaired by their intense personal dislike of each other. Historian Marie Donaghay has chronicled in detail the frustrations, vexations, and mistakes surrounding the implementation of the Anglo-French Commercial Treaty. Her analyses of the post-treaty negotiations over procedures and her discussions about the collateral reforms required to implement the treaty combine to tell a tale of hesitancy, disarray, and a rising sense of betrayal on both sides of the Channel.[17]

The British complained that the way the French measured the capacity of a hogshead of wine shortchanged British importers. When the French used weight to set the value of certain British fabrics entering France, the British objected—and the French on second thought agreed—that this meant that finer, lighter fabrics entered at a lower evaluation than coarse, heavier cloths. Each side was determined to limit severely the raw materials exported to the other if they thought they could help their own manufacturers and

16. Marie Donaghay, "The Best Laid Plans: French Execution of the Anglo-French Commercial Treaty of 1786," *European History Quarterly* 14 (1984): 401.

17. Marie Donaghay, "The Vicious Circle: The Anglo-French Commercial Treaty of 1786 and the Dutch Crisis of 1787," a paper delivered at the annual meeting of the Consortium on Revolutionary Europe in Tallahassee, Florida, Fall 1989.

hurt the manufacturers of the other. The tariff reforms the French had planned to ease the progress of the commercial treaty never materialized. Some of the conflicts over implementation had roots in the French financial crisis. France had to restrict the number of ports opened to British trade because it could not afford the costs of maintaining a large number of well-trained customs officials in all ports. A French promise to reimburse British merchants when their packages of goods from Britain were seized in disputes about value or content was not kept, because of the shortage of money. At times, payment was delayed so long that British merchants felt they were being cheated.[18]

As the English and French ministers labored with the countless vexations associated with the implementation of the Anglo-French Commercial Treaty, other issues of European and non-European dimensions drew the two nations into the dangerous waters of diplomatic and military conflict. The crisis in the Dutch Republic, the subject of the next chapter, was the most dramatic example of these issues. When the British and the Prussians cooperated with the Stadholder in the Dutch Republic, not only to defeat French interests there, but to accompany the defeat with a public humiliation of France, the trust and good intentions so essential to the completion of the task of implementing the Anglo-French Commercial Treaty vanished. Not only did the treaty suffer, but so did other pending agreements and conventions between Versailles and London, some of them already tainted with indelible traces of ancient hostilities and official paranoia. A recent settlement over naval buildups, another over the interests of both nations in India as well as potential cooperation in checking Russian expansion in Eastern Europe: all of these issues became more difficult to resolve as trust evaporated. When the Dutch crisis finally ran its course at the end of 1787, France's options regarding the im-

18. Donaghay, "Best Laid Plans," 401–22; see also René Stourm, *Les finances de l'Ancien Régime et de la Révolution* (Paris, 1885), 2:41; Marie Donaghay, "Textiles," 216–17.

plementation of the commercial treaty were severely reduced. And France's financial crisis, now a public spectacle as a result of Louis XVI's rebuff in the Assembly of Notables, made it difficult for customs officials to enforce any agreements that rested on the assumption that government funds would be available. These failures, in turn, reinforced British convictions that France was unreliable, weak, and unable to defend its own fundamental interests.[19]

The defeat in the Dutch Republic provided the context and stimulus for an effective French domestic opposition to the commercial treaty. Critics questioned the government's intentions, condemned its methods, and blamed the negotiators as incompetents. The oppositions's charges and the government's responses opened an acrimonious public debate that went far beyond the merits or demerits of the treaty of commerce and contributed to the general loss of public confidence in the French monarch and his government's capacity to govern.

In August of 1788 a cartoon print appeared in Paris picturing Commerce (symbolized by Mercury) hanged by the neck in a city square. At various places in the picture—on the rope around Mercury's neck, on his feet, etc.—were listed various recent events which, presumably, had brought France to the crisis we now know was a pre-revolutionary crisis. One event in the cartoon was the three-day stock market panic; another was government borrowing, still another "privileges." But the central image was that of Mercury with his hands tied together. The bindings around his wrists contained the telling statement, "The Treaty of Commerce—more than any other abuse, the recent treaty with England has paralyzed French commerce."[20] The Anglo-French Commercial Treaty of

19. The most thorough discussion of the relation between the Dutch crisis and the implementation of the Anglo-French Commercial Treaty are Marie Donaghay, "Best Laid Plans," 414–15, and "Trust Misplaced: Anglo-French Relations after Vergennes," an unpublished paper delivered at the annual meeting of the Southern Historical Association at Orlando, Florida, 11–13 November 1993.

20. A detailed description of the cartoon is in Charles Schmidt, "La crise industrielle de 1788 en France," *Revue Historique* 97 (January–April 1908): 78.

1786, these critics all agreed, was the cause of the devastating re-cession that plagued the French economy in 1786–87. It threat-ened, they said, the very existence of French manufacturers and re-duced French workers to unemployment and poverty. A recent hail storm had ruined crops in Champagne and Normandy, one critic noted, but that was an act of God and no one could be blamed for that. But the treaty was not an act of God; it was an act of the government. Louis XVI and his ministers, consequently, were responsible.

In Troyes, in the Champagne region, the textiles manufacturers protested to the king's intendant that raw materials were scarce or no longer available because they were being bought up by foreign-ers (read "Britons") entering France under the terms of the com-mercial treaty. But the most vehement condemnations in the peti-tion of protest were reserved for the terms of the Anglo-French Commercial Treaty, which allegedly allowed the British to flood French markets, thereby forcing manufacturers to lay off almost 2000 workers in the region. Unemployed workers were leaving their homes and becoming homeless drifters, moving from pro-vince to province, carrying with them an undefined but apparently sinister "spirit of independence." Even worse, other unemployed were leaving France altogether and going to countries where they were eagerly welcomed because of their technical skills. Poverty was so widespread in Champagne that the archbishop complained to the controller general of the region's inability to cope with the "30,000 poor" and begged him to approach the king for charity. But the king's purse was empty, the controller général responded. There was no money for charity. In Sedan, in December of 1787, the royal drapers called an assembly to assess the alleged destruc-tion caused by the commercial treaty and to discuss how they could organize sufficient alms to provide, at least, the "basic needs of the unemployed." They also petitioned the controller general for aid. They received the same answer sent to Troyes: the royal treasury had no money. In any case, the controller général responded, charity only encouraged idleness.[21]

The chamber of commerce of Rouen launched a campaign to demonstrate to French public opinion how the ills of the economy originated in the treaty of commerce and how the treaty was a glaring example of the disgraceful French submission to British domination. The chamber of commerce began with a weak assurance that it did not blame Louis XVI for the ruin of the French textile industry. But it wanted the public to know that the people who were destined to suffer the most from the commercial treaty were never consulted and did not even know about the agreement until it was signed. Other manufacturers or their spokesmen agreed: Louis XVI's ministers made a treaty with insufficient information because they did not confer with the interested parties. One critic even claimed that the treaty was concluded "clandestinely."[22] Marie Donaghay has persuasively contradicted such charges with evidence that the information gathering and consultations on the part of the French were as thorough as those in Britain and in some cases even more thorough.[23]

The chamber of commerce of Rouen then went on to paint a bleak picture of its textile industry. Before the Portuguese signed the Methuen Treaty with the British in 1703, claimed the chamber of commerce, Portugal had enjoyed a healthy woolen industry along with a flourishing merchant marine. But the treaty with the British sent the Portuguese economy and even the Portuguese population into decline. The same could happen in France if the

21. Ibid., 79–82.

22. Quoted in Jules de Vroil, "Le traité de commerce de 1786," *Journal des Economistes* 17 (1870): 57.

23. On the information and consultations on the part of the French in preparation for negotiating and implementng the treaty see Marie Donaghay, "Calonne and the Anglo-French Commercial Treaty of 1786," *Journal of Modern History* 50 (1978). University Microfilms U-00038. Also by the same author: "Textiles," 218–20; "The Exchange of Products of the Soil," 401.

commercial treaty allowed Britain to invade the French economy.[24] Public opinion was encouraged to believe that the Anglo-French Commercial Treaty and the French ministers who negotiated it were responsible for the "ruin" of the French textile industry, the recession that accompanied it, and the eventual "domination" of France by Britain.

In February of 1788 the principal minister, Loménie de Brienne, called a meeting of the members of the recently revived bureau of commerce to discuss what to do about the economic crisis. Among the invited guests assembled around the table were farmers' generals, councillors of state, the secretary of state for foreign affairs, the minister of the navy, the controller general, members of the bureau of commerce, and assorted notables of the realm and of the colonies. Having dined lavishly at a cornucopian table, this impressive array of talent and power then discussed the economic crisis and the problems of an estimated 200,000 unemployed workers. According to Tolozan, the intendant of commerce, the unemployed were only the most visible victims of the ruinous Anglo-French Commercial Treaty. Among the unanswered questions confronting these unemployed was how they, their wives, and their children were going to survive without the wherewithal to buy food. As Tolozan's audience digested the implications of this after-dinner question, the intendant went on to describe the human costs of economic disorder. And what was the foremost cause of such misery?[25]

The answer, articulated in Tolozan's speech and echoed throughout the realm was unanimous: the Anglo-French Commercial Treaty of 1786. Yes, Italian manufacturers were once again producing goods that successfully competed with French goods. And yes, the Germans had slapped duties on French materials in order to protect German producers. And yes, French and Spanish con-

24. Donaghay, "The Vicious Circle," 12.
25. Schmidt, "La crise Industrielle," 82–84.

sumers seemed to be buying less than usual. But the fundamental cause of economic hardship was "that fatal treaty with England, the death decree for French manufactures."[26] Opposition to trade with Britain became so vocal that British merchants found it increasingly difficult to sell their goods in France, because enraged French manufacturers and workers warned that they would destroy—in open violation of the treaty—any shops that carried goods imported from Britain. In Lyon, the mayor, responding to pressure from local shopkeepers, prohibited cutlery and hardware shippers from advertising English wares.[27]

Beginning in 1785 and continuing through 1788, France without question suffered from a punishing recession. Furthermore, the progress of the recession coincided with the signing and implementation of the commercial treaty. Consequently, in the public mind the two events were connected. But in fact, the relationship was not as simple as the critics implied. In some regions of France the presence of British goods probably intensified an already serious economic crisis. Certainly the fear of British competition may have lowered the confidence levels of some French manufactures. But in Paris, for example, the recession peaked in mid-1786, before the treaty was signed. At the same time, there were regional crises unrelated to the treaty. A superabundance of grapes sharply reduced prices, severe weather cut grain harvests and sharp rises in the price of grain increased hunger.[28] And whatever the economic trends, there were always pockets of stagnation, decline, poverty, and bankruptcies. Thus severe contractions in France's economy left thousands of people out of work and adrift. But the argument of Tolozan and many others who claimed that France suffered

26. Ibid., 90–93.

27. Donaghay, "The Best Laid Plans," 421–22, n. 94. The participation of shopkeepers and workers in opposition indicates that, in this case at least, "public opinion" included more than the literate elite.

28. Jean-Pierre Poussou, "Le dynamisme de l'economie française sous Louis XVI," *Revue Economique* 40, no. 6 (1989), 965–84.

solely because of the Anglo-French Commercial Treaty was drawn from conclusions unfettered by facts and only vaguely related to reality. Such claims fed the fears of public opinion.

In an anonymous *Letter to the Chamber of Commerce of Normandy* (1788) Dupont de Nemours tried to enlighten the critics. The decline of French tanneries, he said, began before the treaty was signed. Prior to the agreement, changes in fashion reduced sales of some French fabrics. Several manufacturers, DuPont claimed, were simply charging too much and, therefore, were losing their customers. Some of the British goods entering France after the treaty were the same goods that had entered before the treaty as contraband and, consequently, they could hardly have "flooded" the markets. The "flooding" had occurred years before. In the negotiations for the treaty, Rayneval, the French secretary, noted, "I know that in the [pre-treaty] state of things, English contraband flooded France and there was no effective way to stop it." One of the hoped-for advantages of the treaty, according to Rayneval, was that they could substitute legitimate trade for smuggling.[29] These and other official justifications of the government's commercial treaty kept the clerks busy and the presses rolling. But the government's explanations were long and complicated, filled with endless details and dry reasoning. They did little to change the public judgment.[30]

The easily grasped charge that the Anglo-French Commercial Treaty was to blame for France's economic troubles stuck in the public memory and played a part in the steady loss of confidence in

29. Quoted in Cahen, "Une nouvelle interprétation," 278.

30. On the debate over the economic consequences of the Anglo-French Commercial Treaty see: *Observations de la chambre de commerce de Normandie sur le Traité . . . entre la France et l'Angleterre* (Rouen, 1788); Henri Sée, "The Normandy Chamber of Commerce and the Commercial Treaty of 1786," *Economic History Review* 2 (1929–30): 308–13; Anonymous [Dupont de Nemours], *Lettre à la Chambre de Commerce de Normandie* (Rouen et Paris, 1788); Charles Schmidt, "La crise industrielle," 78–94; Léon Cahen, "Une nouvelle interpretation," 271–85.

the government. The charge even turned up in the *cahiers de doléances* composed on the eve of the Revolution. In the *cahiers* of the clergy of Beauvais, the priests laid before their monarch the complaint that the treaty had been a harsh blow to the French drapery industry. And it was, the priests explained, the work of persons with no practical experience, who were seduced by the false, erroneous and "brilliant theories [of the physiocrats]."[31] In 1789, another critic of the treaty, one Boyetet, an official of the government, compared France to an exhausted man weakened from being surgically bled from all four limbs. And that, Boyetet said, "was . . . the effect of that fatal treaty the government contracted without deigning to consult the Nation."[32] How, indeed, could public opinion honor a government of men so indifferent to vital French interests and so obviously responsible for the economic ills that plagued France? After defeating Britain in the War for American Independence, France seemingly had surrendered without a struggle to a devastating invasion of British merchants and shopkeepers. Unfortunately, the public's misconceptions about the commercial treaty were only a part of the widespread erosion of respect for the monarchy. When a long-simmering diplomatic crisis exploded in the Dutch Republic, the public in France once again plunged into a heated debate over whether the government had lost its direction and its nerve.

31. Schmidt, "La crise industrielle," 93; Cahen, "Une nouvelle interprétation," 271.

32. Cahen, "Une nouvelle interprétation," 285.

The Dutch Disaster: 1783–1788

T HE DUTCH, according to a French publicist of the eighteenth century, "are afraid of everyone, suffer everything,
complain of everything and guarantee nothing."[1] During
the American Revolutionary War, the Dutch Republic abandoned
a half-century of neutrality in European squabbles and entered the
war on the side of France, Spain, and the United States. But the
new allies never got along. Louis XVI and members of his cabinet
were exasperated by what they perceived as the passiveness of the
Dutch fleet during the war. At the peace table, the Dutch were in
turn bitterly disappointed that Louis XVI supported only a few of
their demands. But the American Revolutionary War changed the
balance of a long-standing constitutional conflict in the Dutch Republic. The Dutch Patriot party emerged from the war with renewed influence and vigor. Their traditional enemy, the Orangist
party, led by the stadholder, William V, suffered an eclipse of pub-

1. Jean-Louis Favier, "Conjectures raisonnées sur la situation actuelle de la
France dans le systême politique de l'Europe," printed in *Politique de tous les cabi-
nets de l'Europe pendant les règnes de Louis XV et Louis XVI* (Paris, 1793), 1:255. There
are several good treatments of the Dutch crisis of 1787. See: Jonathan Israel, *The
Dutch Republic: Its Rise, Greatness and Fall, 1477–1806* (Oxford, 1995); Jeremy
Black, *British Foreign Policy in an Age of Revolution* (Cambridge, 1994); Simon
Schama, *Patriots and Liberators: Revolution in the Netherlands, 1788–1813* (New
York, 1977).

lic favor. The situation soon developed into a profound constitutional crisis. The stadholder, the chief magistrate of the Dutch Republic, historically enjoyed strong support from Britain, but the wartime depredations and humiliations suffered by the Dutch at the hands of the British navy and diplomats created much bitterness in the Republic. Furthermore, the British-Dutch negotiations for peace raised for the Dutch the painful vision of diplomatic isolation. The Patriots turned to France, therefore, for support against the stadholder. They hoped to cement an alliance with Louis XVI that would protect them from from British interference while they accomplished their domestic agenda.[2]

The French ambassador to the Hague supported the Patriots and favored an alliance. The French secretary of state for the navy, the maréchal de Castries, also supported it, because he believed an alliance would bring into a powerful combination the Dutch, French and, with the Family Compact, the Spanish fleets. Such a league, Castries hoped, would provide France with the military might to win yet another naval war against Britain and consolidate France's newly won diplomatic position as well as begin the dislodgement of Britain in India.[3] Louis XVI's secretary of state for

2. "Propositions de plénipotentiaires Hollandais, 23 June, 1783"; Bérenger to Vergennes, 13 June, 3 October 1783, AAE-cp-Hollande, 554:346ff., 556:6; LaVauguyon to Vergennes, 23, 27, 30 April 1784," ibid., 557:431ff., 443ff., 462ff. On the question of Franco-Dutch wartime relations, see the correspondence between Vergennes and LaVauguyon in AAE-cp-Hollande, especially vols. 543 to 552. The minister of the navy, Castries felt the Dutch were difficult to deal with. See his notes and letters in ibid., especially 548:175vo-176, 220–23, 224–25, 236–40, 291, and 315–315vo, and 549:89–89vo; Orville T. Murphy, *Charles Gravier, Comte de Vergennes: French Diplomacy in the Age of Revolution, 1719–1987* (Albany, N.Y., 1982), 459–63.

3. LaVauguyon's position in favor of a Dutch treaty is expressed several times in AAE-cp-Hollande, 557:431ff.; 443ff.; 462ff. Ambassador Breteuil and Calonne's favorable attitude toward a Dutch alliance is expressed in a "Mémoire," in ibid., "Supplement," 21:103ff. See also Alfred Cobban, *Ambassadors and Secret Agents* (London, 1954), 26; Duc de Castries, *Le Maréchal de Castries: serviteur de trois rois, 1727–1800* (Paris, 1979), 113.

"Rehearsal," by the Hanoverian artist Johann Henrich Ramberg: The doughty Dutch burghers, assisted by their allies, the French "frogs," stand firm against a moustached caricature of a Prussian soldier sketched on a stone wall. Copyright © the British Museum, reproduced by permission.

foreign affairs, Vergennes, hesitated before the prospect of a Dutch alliance. He felt that any negotiations must include the stadholder and other representatives of Dutch political and commercial interests as well as the Patriot party. Also, he was not impressed with the Dutch as allies. Dutch naval inactivity during the war left him unconvinced of their will to fight.[4] His estimate was confirmed later when Dutch resistance to the invasion of Prussia crumbled soon after Prussian troops crossed the border. Consequently, in

4. A discussion of Vergennes's reservations and attitude toward the Dutch alliance is in Murphy, *Vergennes*, 465–71.

1784 when Joseph II provoked a conflict with the Dutch Republic over navigation of the Scheldt River, Vergennes postponed discussion about agreements with the Dutch while Louis XVI mediated Dutch-Austrian differences. Nevertheless, Louis XVI eventually was persuaded to accept the Dutch alliance because of the obvious value of such an alliance in closing one more door to British influence in Europe. In addition, the Patriots included among their numbers Dutch bankers and brokers who were withdrawing investments from Britain and were eager to invest in French securities at the very moment the French state needed loans.[5]

Thus, in 1785 Louis XVI and the Dutch Republic signed a defensive alliance. Immediately, the many potential disadvantages of the alliance surfaced. Louis XVI soon began to doubt the wisdom of supporting the Patriots when he learned more about their liberal political ideals. It was one thing to support Republicans in faraway America; it was another thing to encourage them so close to home. He would rather give up the alliance, he warned, "than give Holland over to a pure democracy."[6]

In 1786 a new agent changed the chemistry of Dutch politics. Frederick William II succeeded Frederick II (the Great) on the Prussian throne. Frederick William II was the brother of the Dutch stadholder's wife, and he felt honor bound to support his sister, the Princess of Orange, and her husband, William V, even though Prussia had no vital interests at stake in the Dutch Republic.[7] Apparently he gave support to his sister, at least at first, thinking that the French connection with the Patriots would provide a tight reign on the extravagances of that party. Louis XVI seems also to have believed he could restrain the Patriots. Moreover,

5. J. C. Riley, "Dutch Investment in France, 1781–1787," *Journal of Economic History* 33, no. 4 (December 1973), 733–35.

6. Quoted in Pierre de Witt, *Une invasion prussienne en Hollande en 1787* (Paris, 1896), 186.

7. T. C. W. Blanning, *The Origins of the French Revolutionary Wars* (London and New York, 1986), 52.

Louis XVI counted on his traditional influence in Berlin to ensure Frederick William's acceptance of whatever developed in the Dutch Republic. But Versailles misjudged its allies. At the same time, it underestimated the abilities of James Harris, the British ambassador at The Hague, and the persistence of Frederick William's adviser Count Ewald Friedrich von Hertzberg.

Harris crossed the Channel to the Continent determined to revive the stadholder's cause and defeat the Patriots.[8] Moreover, Harris, with Carmarthen, the British foreign secretary, was a warm advocate in the British government of a close alliance with Prussia. In the spring of 1785 Harris had been instrumental in the decision of George III (as the elector of Hanover) to adhere to Prussia's *Furstenbund*.

The last foreign minister to serve under Frederick II, von Hertzberg was an experienced statesman when Frederick William II came to the throne in 1786. He had helped draw up the peace treaties between Prussia and Russia and between Prussia and Sweden when the Seven Years' War drew to a close. But his growing differences with Frederick II over policy, especially Frederick's participation in the First Partition of Poland (which Hertsberg thought was impolitic), reduced his influence with the Prussian king. But soon after Frederick William's reign began in 1786, Hertzberg received an approving nod from the new king. He was convinced that Prussian power and interests in Europe could best be served by a "Northern League" which brought Britain and Prussia into alliance with the Dutch Republic, Denmark, and, possibly, Russia. While the Russian actor in his plans refused to sign on, a key element in Hertzberg's script materialized when the political crisis in the Dutch Republic brought Harris to The Hague. Harris, as we have seen, also wanted a Prussian alliance.

By 1791 Hertzberg's "Plan" had foundered on his own miscon-

8. Harris's active role in this diplomatic episode is narrated in Alfred Cobban, *Ambassadors and Secret Agents*.

ceptions, one of which was that Great Britain would be willing to support Prussia's ambition to change the map of Eastern Europe with a series of treaties between Prussia, the Ottoman Empire, Austria, and Poland. For Prussia, the result of this dexterous shuffle was to be the acquisition of the cities of Thorn and Danzig, the Palatinate of Posen, and the Polish manufacturing town of Kalisch. But in 1787, Hertzberg's "Plan" did not yet seem the fantasy it turned out to be. And Frederick William II, convinced that family honor required that he support his sister in the Dutch Republic, also saw in the Dutch situation the opportunity to achieve an alliance with Britain. Intervention in Dutch politics seemed a fair price to pay to expand Prussian power and territory, even if the price included war.[9]

William Pitt tried at first to avoid any action in the Dutch Republic that might require British military intervention. But as the conflict between the stadholder and the Patriots heated up in the spring of 1787, it became more difficult for Britain to remain neutral. The French envoy, Vérac, was actively encouraging the Patriots; the British envoy, Harris—thoroughly committed to the Stadholder's cause—was trying with increasing success to persuade London to recognize the importance of the opportunities in the Dutch Republic. By the end of June 1787, the new French secretary of state for foreign affairs, the comte de Montmorin, recognized that Harris was succeeding.[10]

Pitt finally came around to Harris and Carmarthen's views, which argued for a more vigorous anti-French, anti-Patriot policy in the Dutch Republic.[11] Once assured of British support, the stad-

9. Blanning, *The Origins of the French Revolutionary Wars*, 51–55.

10. Montmorin to Marquis de Vérac, 23 June 1787. AAE-cp-Hollande 573:215.

11. Jeremy Black, "The Marquis of Carmarthen and Relations with France, 1784–1787," *Francia* 12 (1985): 289–309; also, Jeremy Black, "Sir Robert Ainsley: His Majesty's Agent-provocateur? British Foreign Policy and the International Crisis of 1787," *European History Quarterly* 14 (1984): 259.

holder acted. He attacked the city of Utrecht and, in response, the States of Holland organized to resist him. In June, soldiers of the Patriot party briefly detained the princess of Orange. Indignant that the Patriots would presume to interfere with her right to travel, the princess saw the event as a public humiliation. To Frederick William II, the king of Prussia, the public insult to his sister wounded his family and diplomatic honor. He demanded satisfactions from the States General of the Dutch Republic and immediately approached the British and offered them the chance to support him.

France, now deeply committed to the Patriots, found it impossible to stay clear of the crisis. To meet his obligations to the Dutch, Louis XVI ordered the formation of a troop encampment at Givet, in northeastern France. But Louis, preoccupied with the deteriorating financial crisis at home, found himself face to face with the tough question of whether France could really afford to pay the price of a military operation to aid the Dutch. Worse still, as the crisis in the Dutch Republic developed, it began to take on the ugly appearance of a nightmare French statesmen had learned to fear: the possibility of a land war on the Continent and a naval war with Great Britain.

In early August of 1787, Montmorin held a series of discussions with British representatives at Versailles, in which they talked about the Dutch affair and how to bring about a suspension of the hostilities. He was especially anxious to discuss ways to reduce the risks of a war involving France and Britain. In the course of their conversations, they even discussed the wisdom of the French army encampment at Givet and explored whether or not they could agree on some measure of naval disarmament. But if Frederick William's troops moved to invade the Dutch Republic, Louis XVI warned, French troops would march to defend them. France did not want the Prussians to dictate a settlement of the Dutch crisis. Nor did Britain, the British diplomats responded, want France to dictate a settlement.

The diplomatic correspondence recording these conversations suggests that for a short time Louis XVI and George III were, in fact, dealing with each other frankly and in a way calculated to reduce suspicion and build trust. By late August, George III and Louis XVI agreed to a Project for Disarmament, in which they promised to discontinue the scheduled increases in their navies. If either power found itself obliged to go back on the commitment, they promised, it would notify the other in advance.[12] Soon after, when an ambiguity in the peace treaty of 1783 threatened to create a dispute between the two monarchs over the French East India Company's right to carry on commerce in salt, saltpeter, and opium in India, Montmorin and Eden negotiated an Explanatory Convention and promptly settled the issue.[13]

Montmorin believed he had received a promise from Frederick William II that he would not invade Holland, but by late August 1787, the Prussian king's repeated insistence on "satisfactions" for the insult to his sister made the French secretary of state morally certain that Frederick would invade. That move, Montmorin warned, would change "entirely the state of things." From London the French representative, Barthélemy, reported his suspicions that British preparations indicated it was ready to use the navy to assist Prussia. In a dispatch, Barthélemy articulated what Montmorin and Louis XVI feared most: France could not act forcefully on land against Prussia without being drawn into a naval war with Britain.[14] The two powers, Barthélemy later concluded, now acted

12. "Declaration," approved by Louis XVI, 17 August 1787, and officially dated 30 August 1787. AAE-cp-Angleterre, 561:134. Printed in Georg Frederic de Martens, *Recueil des principaux traités . . . conclus par les puissances de l'Europe . . .* (Gottinque, 1826), 2d ed., 5:277.

13. "Explanatory Convention between France and Great Britain, signed at Versailles, 31 August 1787. Printed in Clive Parry, ed., *Consolidated Treaty Series* (Dobbs Ferry, N.Y., 1969), 50:213.

14. Barthelemy to Montmorin, 14 and ? August, 1787, AAE-cp-Angleterre, 561:55; 563:27–28, 67. Quoted in ibid., 536.

in "intimate concert."[15] In a last-minute attempt to get the Prussian king to stop military preparations, Montmorin sent a special envoy, the baron de Groschlag, to Berlin. But Groschlag failed. The Prussian king, he reported on his return to France, "considers France absolutely incapable of sustaining at the same time a land war and a sea war.[16]

As the Dutch crisis deepened, Harris's ceaseless activities and Carmarthen's deep-seated distrust of France triumphed.[17] Britain decided to reestablish the stadholder with powers the Patriots were determined he should not have. William Pitt, having talked with Calonne, who fled to London after his dismissal as Louis XVI's controller general, concluded that the pitiful state of French finances severely limited Louis XVI's power to act. That news increased the likelihood of success if Britain intervened.[18] In the midst of these developments, news arrived that the Ottoman Empire and Russia were on the verge of war. If Russia warred with the Turks, Frederick William II was free to act in Holland without fear of a Russian attack from the east. The French ambassador at Constantinople was convinced that the Turks now wanted a war, and he firmly believed that the British were behind their change of heart.[19] Louis XVI's unsteady confidence in Britain's goodwill began to fade. Why should Britain stand by and let the French-backed Dutch Patriots challenge the British-backed statholder when France was paralyzed with a political crisis? When Louis

15. Barthelemy to Montmorin, 20 August, 1787, AAE-cp-Angleterre, 561:76. Cited in ibid.

16. Albert Waddington, ed., *Recueil des Instructions donnés aux ambassadeurs et ministres . . .* (Paris, 1901), Prusse, 16:567.

17. Jeremy Black, "The Marquis of Carmarthen," 285.

18. Ibid., 299–300.

19. Ali Ihsan Bagis, "The Embassy of Sir Robert Ainsley at Istanbul (1776–1794)" (unpublished Ph.D. thesis, University of London, 1974), 17–18. For further discussion of Ainsley's role in the Turkish declaration of war see Jeremy Black, "Sir Robert Ainsley," 253–83.

XVI saw Britain in a similar vulnerable position before the War of the American Revolution, he did not hesitate to take advantage of Britain's embarrassment. Could Louis expect George III to do otherwise?

On the 13th of September Prussia took advantage of the strategic opportunities provided by a Russo-Turkish war and invaded the Dutch Republic. The British repeatedly denied they had any part in the Turks' decision to go to war, but the rumors and suspicions did their damage. Whatever bridge of trust Louis XVI and George III had so carefully built now buckled and collapsed. The French minister in London, Barthélemy, concluded that Britain wanted—and deliberately planned—to humiliate France and detach it from its new ally, the Dutch Republic.[20] On the 22nd of September, in accordance with the Project of Disarmament agreed upon barely a month before, Britain informed France of its intention to resume increasing its naval armaments. The next day, Carmarthen informed Louis XVI that if France sent troops into Holland in response to the Prussian invasion, "war would be inevitable."

Meanwhile, at Versailles, members of Louis XVI's council angrily disputed what France should do. The secretaries of state for the army and the navy, Ségur and Castries, energetically argued for immediately marching twenty-five battalions to the northern frontier to call Frederick Williams's bluff.[21] They knew that such a decision almost certainly would lead to another French war with Britain, with Prussia as Great Britain's ally. But Ségur and Castries were prepared to accept that scenario. Castries personally wanted another war with Britain, because he believed it would assure French hegemony in Europe and open the way toward in-

20. Paul Vaucher, ed., *Recueil des instructions données aux ambassadeurs et ministres de France depuis les traités de Westphalie jusqu'à la révolution français* (Paris, 1965), vol. 25, Angleterre, 2, tome III, 536.

21. Baron de Besenval, *Mémoires de M. le Baron de Besenval* (Paris, 1805), 3:286–87; Castries, *Maréchal de Castries*, 129–32; Comte de Ségur, *Le Maréchal de Ségur*, 315–16.

creasing French power in India at Britain's expense.[22] But the principal minister, Loménie de Brienne, with the support of the queen, the secretary of state for foreign affairs, Montmorin, and the master of the royal household, Malsherbes, strongly opposed intervention.[23]

The major consideration of those who opposed war was the terrible disorder of French finances. Equally disturbing was the fact that the political crisis over state finances generated intense and passionate public discussion at home. What had begun as a financial crisis and had become a foreign policy crisis was now a revolutionary crisis. The government of France was at a stalemate. News from Constantinople confirmed that war between France's old friend the Ottoman Empire and France's new friend Russia was now a reality. France's ally, the Austrian Empire, was also allied with Russia and divided about what to do about the declining Turks.[24] Louis XVI knew France's repeated refusals to support any of Joseph II's moves against the Turks would make Austria a very demanding, if not unreliable, ally, should France go to war in the Dutch Republic and ask for help. France was not even certain it could count on the help of its Spanish ally. But above all, the specter of fighting a naval war and a land war simultaneously could not be exorcized by Ségur and Castries's militant sword rattling. Louis XVI's estimate of what France was capable of achieving persuaded him to do nothing. Moreover, as the French cabinet argued the matter, the time needed to prepare and march the French soldiers to defend the Dutch ticked away.[25] Finally, on the 22nd of September, Louis XVI informed the Patriots that France could not help them.[26] Fred-

22. Duc de Castries, *Maréchal de Castries*, 113, 129

23. Jean Egret, *The French Prerevolution: 1787–1788* (Chicago, 1977), 40–42; L. P. Ségur, *Mémoires ou Souvenirs et Anecdotes* (Paris, 1843), 2:280–81.

24. Karl Roider, *Austria's Eastern Question: 1700–1790* (Princeton, 1982), 194.

25. Besenval, *Mémoires*, 3:287.

26. "Instructions to Saint Priest, 14 September, 1787." Printed in *Receuil des Instructions données aux ambassadeur et ministres de France depuis les traités de Westphalie jusqu'à la révolution française*, Holland, 3:415.

erick William II's Prussian army was already camping on Dutch soil. Pleased with the turn of events, Harris, Carmarthen, and von Hertzberg watched the unfolding of their plans for a solid, anti-French Anglo-Prussian alliance.

While French ministers disagreed, young General Lafayette, responding to Dutch initiatives, agreed to organize unofficial support for the Patriots. Still enjoying the role of hero of the American Revolution, Lafayette believed that the Dutch situation offered startling parallels with the early stages of the American Revolution.[27] Were not the Patriots in the Dutch Republic also defending their "liberties"? And once again, France's bitter enemy, Britain, opposed liberty. Lafayette discussed with Dutch agents the possibility of assuming command of a force of some twenty thousand volunteers who would defend the Patriots' cause. During the secret discussions, the Dutch even held out the possibility that "as soon as affairs grew serious" Lafayette might become the head of all the military forces of the Dutch Republic.[28]

Louis XVI played no official role in this intrigue, but both Loménie de Brienne and the maréchal de Castries knew about it.[29] The plan was sabotaged, according to Lafayette, by Vérac, the French ambassador to the Dutch Republic. Vérac's candidate for the command of the twenty thousand volunteers was not Lafayette but the rhinegrave of Salm. Vérac, still according to Lafayette, persuaded the Dutch that Louis XVI did not want Lafayette to head the volunteers, and the rhinegrave of Salm received the command. Surprised and deeply resentful of Vérac's intervention, Lafayette expressed his anger in a letter to his dear friend George Washington: the rhinegrave, he said was a "cowardly adventurer [sic]." Vérac blundered and deceived everyone, he told Washington. Worse still,

27. Louis Gottschalk, *Lafayette between the American and the French Révolution (1783–1789)* (Chicago, 1950), 338.
28. Lafayette to George Washington, 9 October 1787, in Louis Gottschalk, ed., *The Letters of Lafayette to Washington: 1777–1779* (New York, 1944), 331.
29. Ibid., 331.

Lafayette lamented, the diplomatic crisis had paralyzed the French government. Only Britain "gained in the bargain."[30]

Lafayette was not the only noble military officer outraged by Louis XVI's refusal to march French troops into the Dutch Republic. To many of them, the decision to avoid war was pure and simply an act of cowardice. Forgetting the financial problems or possible military consequences, many military officers argued that their own personal honor as well as Louis XVI's honor was at stake. In 1788, army officers at the military camp of the prince de Condé openly and "without pity" berated and exaggerated the perceived disarray at Versailles and loudly praised those who opposed the decisions of the king.[31] This disaffection of the military was not a cause of the Revolution, the journalist Rivarol believed, "it *was* the Revolution."[32] Louis's decision not to enter the war to support the Dutch only confirmed the opinion of the king's brother, the comte de Provence, that the weakness and indecision of the king were now beyond words.[33]

The secretaries of state for the navy and army, the maréchal de Castries and the maréchal de Ségur, doggedly opposed the decision to abandon the Dutch. Castries's dissatisfaction with French foreign policy was of long standing, and the Dutch affair was vinegar on old wounds. In 1783, Castries had fiercely opposed the peace settlement Vergennes was cautiously arranging to close the War of the American Revolution. Castries had wanted France to keep the conquests it made at the expense of the British during the war, but Vergennes had sacrificed them in the hopes of a *rapprochement* with Britain. In 1786, as the crisis in the Dutch Republic boiled over, Castries renewed the battle with a blistering attack on Vergennes. Reading aloud in the king's council, he reopened the

30. Louis Gottschalk, *Lafayette between the American and the French Revolution*, 340–41.

31. Albert Sorel, *L'Europe et la Révolution Française* (Paris, 1885), 1:214.

32. Cited in ibid., 1:214.   33. Ibid., 1:210.

"Performance," by the Hanoverian artist Johann Heinrich Ramberg: A burlesque of what really happened. Note the "frogs" escaping from the scene. Copyright © the British Museum, reproduced by permission.

debate over the peace of 1783 and he condemned Vergennes's handling of foreign affairs from the very moment he had become secretary of state for foreign affairs. Vergennes was guilty of every character flaw Castries could think of: timidity, cowardice, failing to take advantage of opportunities, and repeated bad judgment. He even accused Vergennes of having learned bad diplomatic habits (i.e., falseness and finesse) from the Turks during the time he had been France's ambassador to Constantinople. In Eastern Europe, Castries complained, Vergennes never could think of anything to do but offer France's mediation. The French response to the Dutch debacle, Castries fumed, was simply a continuation of Vergennes's failed policies. The Dutch episode, Castries said, could be France's moment to deal once and for all with the Dutch stadholder. Instead, France caved in and failed to stand up to the king of Prussia. It was no longer possible, Castries argued, to hide the "rapid degradation of France's credit, consideration and dignity."[34]

Outside the ministries and cabinets, others echoed the charges. The baron de Besenval found France's inaction shameful. It illustrated, he thought, the "usual cowardice" of the king's ministry.[35] The young Alexandre de Lameth, concerned about the king's slipping authority, wanted France to plunge into war as a desperate way to save France. A war, he thought, would bolster the king's power, since the *gloire* and honor associated with war would divert attention from the messy problems at home and bring the military aristocracy around to supporting the king. Lameth seemed unconcerned that war was a heavy price to pay for the loyalty of the aristocracy. Also, war would have derailed all the plans for financial reform. Brienne, though, brought the discussion back to the harsh realities: "France was in no position to interfere in the quarrels of her neighbors."[36] Thus, Louis XVI watched and did nothing as Prussia crushed the Patriots. The survivors fled the Dutch Republic by the thousands, most of them to France, where they lived on into the French Revolution as a demoralized, quarrelsome, and poverty-stricken exile community surviving on the charities of the French government.[37] Meanwhile, Louis XVI braced himself for

34. Quoted in Jean-François Labourdette, *Vergennes, Ministre principal de Louis XVI* (Paris, 1990), 284–90.

35. Besenval, *Mémoires*, 3:295.

36. Jean Egret, *The French Pre-revolution*, 40–42; Lafayette to George Washington, 9 October 1787, *The Letters of Lafayette to George Washington: 1777–1799*, 329, 332; the statement by Brienne is quoted by Egret from: Duc de Levi, *Souvenirs et portraits (1780–1789)* (Paris, 1813), 110–11.

37. R. van Gelder, "Patriotten in Ballingschap, 1787–1795," *Spiegel Hist.* (Netherlands) 14, no. 2 (1979), 80–87.

the public backlash that would surely accompany the diplomatic defeat.

From the perspective of history, the decision to stay out of the war seems the most prudent and responsible choice in the face of the financial and political crisis at home. But in the opinion of many contemporaries, it was clearly a shameful and public humiliation for France. The Prussian minister to London, Count von Hertzberg, expressed the opinion of Europe: "Along with having lost the alliance with Holland, France has lost the last of its prestige...."[38]

Meanwhile, Louis's government fell apart. Castries resigned and Ségur soon followed. Now, with a weakened and badly divided ministry, Louis XVI tried to cope with a major diplomatic disgrace, a financial collapse, a rebellion of his Parlement, and the discontent of an important and vocal segment of the French military and aristocratic elite. To his minister to the United States, Louis tried to explain the events in Holland as the result of pure chance. Impossible to foresee, he said. He did not intervene, he continued, because he did not want to deliver the Dutch Republic over to a civil war and provoke at the same time a general war in Europe.[39] But court opinion saw him as weak and turning more and more to the queen for guidance. The Swede Axel Fersen actually believed that Louis acted only with the consent of the queen. "He trusts only the queen," Fersen wrote, "and it appears that it is she who does everything."[40] Such was the image of the man designated by Divine Right to lead France.

38. Quoted in Vaucher, ed., *Receuil des instructions*, 538.

39. "Mémoire pour servir d'Instruction au Sieur Comte de Moustier, Chevalier de l'Ordre royal et militaire de St. Louis allant en Amérique en qualité de Ministre Plénipotentiaire du Roi près du Congrès des Etats-Unis," printed in Henry E. Bourne, "Correspondence of the Comte de Moustier with the Comte de Montmorin, 1787–1789," *American Historical Review* 8 (1902–3): 710–14.

40. Quoted in André Castelot, *Marie Antoinette* (London, 1957), trans. Denise Folliot, 224.

For Prussia and Great Britain the Dutch episode was a major step in a dramatic climb back to a position of influence in Europe. In June of 1788 they signed a provisional treaty at Loo. Two months later they confirmed it with signatures at Berlin. With the treaties that both powers made simultaneously with the Dutch Republic, the new arrangement formed a Triple Alliance, which brought together two major naval powers with a strong land power—the very combination France had learned through harsh experience to fear the most. Clearly, diplomatic sands had shifted.

SEVEN

The United States: 1783–1789

WHEN THE WAR of the American Revolution ended, America's ally Louis XVI decided to keep the Confederation of the United States weak and dependent to assure that it would remain a ward of France. Such was the ardent opinion of the American historian Samuel Flagg Bemis. The Confederation, Bemis said, was a feeble republic and France was "content to see her new client remain in this condition." The comte de Vergennes, Louis XVI's secretary of state for foreign affairs, Bemis concluded, "preferred to see the American Confederation politically too impotent to collect its taxes than strong enough to pay its debts to France and to defend its rights and interest against all comers. He did not want to see the new republic gravitate outside the orbit of French diplomatic control."[1] Today, historians of Franco-American diplomacy hold more moderate opinions of France's intentions. Nevertheless, the opinion still lingers on that France wanted the United States to be weak and dependent.[2]

1. Samuel Flagg Bemis, *A Diplomatic History of the United States* (New York, 1936), 82. For a similar opinion see Clyde Augustus Duniway, "French Influence on the Adoption of the Federal Constitution," *American Historical Review* 9 (Oct. 1903–July 1904), 304–9.

2. For the opinions of more recent historians of Louis XVI's policy toward the American union of Confederation, see for example: Richard W. Leopold, *The Growth of American Foreign Policy* (New York, 1962), 4, 17–18; Thomas A. Bailey,

From 1784 to 1789 France was represented in the United States by Louis Guillaume Otto, comte de Mosloy, and Eléonore-François-Elie, comte de Moustier. Otto was born in Baden in 1754. The son of an old Protestant family, he attended the Protestant University at Strasburg, where he earned a reputation as a brilliant student of foreign languages and international and feudal law. In 1776, La Luzerne, then minister plenipotentiary to Bavaria, chose Otto to be his secretary because of his reputation as a jurist. When La Luzerne was recalled to France, he recommended that Otto remain in Bavaria to continue correspondence with Versailles. In 1779, when La Luzerne became minister to the United States, Otto accompanied him as personal secretary. Otto was named chargé d'affaires in the United States after the departure of La Luzerne in 1784. Otto continued to serve as secretary when Moustier replaced La Luzerne. After the departure of Moustier for France in 1791, Otto once again assumed the responsibilities of chargé d'affaires. He returned to France in December of 1792.[3]

Moustier did not replace La Luzerne as French minister to the United States until January of 1788, although La Luzerne had returned to France nearly four years earlier. He was born in Paris in 1751 and started his career as a soldier. He began his career in the diplomatic service with the help of his brother-in-law, who was the French ambassador to Lisbon. After service in Portugal, Moustier was sent to London in 1783 to represent France in negotiations concerned with Spanish demands at the end of the War of the American Revolution. From London he was sent to the United States to replace La Luzerne. According to one source, Louis XVI

A Diplomatic History of the American People (New York, 1950), 50; Alexander deConde, *A History of American Foreign Policy* (New York, 1963), 47; Lawrence S. Kaplan, *Colonies into Nation: American Diplomacy; 1763–1801* (New York, 1972), 180–81.

3. *Biographie universelle ancienne et moderne* (Paris, 1822), 32:245–48. Peter P. Hill, *French Perceptions of the Early American Republic: 1783–1793* (Philadelphia, 1988), 10–12.

offered him the post of secretary of state for foreign affairs in 1791, an offer he declined.[4]

The correspondence of Otto and Moustier confirms Bemis's opinion that the young Republic was feeble, but there is considerable evidence to contradict the notion that the French were content to see the United States remain that way. Certainly, France considered the fledgling United States a dependent—a ward—during the American Revolution. To ensure victory, France established special trade arrangements with the Americans, supplied and subsidized the American army, underwrote American currency with loans, and sent a fleet and an army expeditionary force to the American continent to support its struggling ally. When the war ended, France neither desired nor could afford to keep the United States at the wartime level of dependency. Consequently, most of the French aid was discontinued.

But the reduction of support was abrupt, leading some Americans to conclude that Louis XVI was now indifferent to the prosperity and needs of his ally. In February of 1788, France's minister to the United States, Moustier, was surprised to hear John Jay report that there was a very strong opinion in the United States that Louis XVI had "withdrawn his interest in the American Republic and did not care whether the new Republic failed or succeeded."[5] Other Americans, Moustier found, also believed France had abandoned them. Moustier's response was that Louis XVI remained favorable to the American cause but, since the peace of 1783, the weakness and incoherence of the American government made it difficult to understand Americans. "I threw all of the blame on them," Moustier reported to Versailles when he discussed American disappointment in France.[6] Moustier's less-public opinion was

4. *Biographie universelle ancienne et moderne*, 30:343–45.

5. Moustier to Montmorin, 12 Feb. 1788, Archives des Affaires Etrangères-correspondance politique-États Unis (hereafter referred to as AAE-cp-EU), 33:30–32vo.

6. Moustier to Montmorin 19 January 1789, ibid., 34:4.

much harsher: the Americans, he concluded, were like spoiled children who continued to make demands on those who treated them with the greatest kindness and consideration.[7]

Few European diplomats would have disagreed with the opinion that in the 1780s the new American nation was a weak power. During the War of the American Revolution, France channeled its aid and influence through the Continental Congress and the military, especially George Washington, to help provide the American central authority with the strength and authority to prosecute the war. As the French minister to the United States later observed, the Americans were held together during the war by fear, George Washington, and the contributions of foreign powers. But when the peace ended that arrangement, the problems of military security, foreign trade, debts, and political unity became those of the sovereign states under the Articles of Confederation. By 1788, the Continental Congress, as French diplomats perceived that institution, was reduced to such weakness that it could only deliberate; it had few means to implement.[8] Nor were the French alone in the opinion that the new nation was weak. "The present constitution," George Washington wrote in 1786, "is inadequate; the superstructure is tottering to its foundation, and without help will bury us in its ruins."[9]

But the objective reality of postwar weakness of the Continental Congress was not the only factor that conditioned French judgments about the United States. Eighteenth-century European experience seemed to confirm the opinion that a republic was weak and unstable by definition. The Polish Republic was wracked by internal disturbances and foreign intervention. While the Venetian Republic had certainly enjoyed a splendid past, in the late eigh-

7. Moustier to Montmorin, 4 August 1788, ibid., 33:244vo.

8. Moustier to Montmorin 8 February 1788, ibid., 33:17.

9. Washington to David Stuart, 19 November 1786, printed in John C. Fitzpatrick, ed., *The Writings of George Washington* (Washington, D.C., 1939), 29:75–77. See also John Jay to Thomas Jefferson, 27 October 1786, in Julian P. Boyd, ed., *The Papers of Thomas Jefferson* (Princeton, 1954), 10:488–89.

teenth century it was perceived in France as having neither "strength nor activity" regarding matters having to do with external affairs.[10] The Swiss Confederation was a loose and weak union with the cantons divided one against the other. Whatever coherence the Swiss Confederation had was maintained by French military and diplomatic intervention and cash subsidies. The Dutch Republic, similarly divided against itself, by 1787 seemed poised to self destruct.[11] All these Republics had weak governments; they were prone to domestic conflict and vulnerable to foreign influences and foreign intervention. Thus, the historical experience of European statesmen of the eighteenth century clearly argued that Republics rarely achieved an independent status in the international arena.[12]

Otto compared the Confederation of the United States to the Polish Republic, which by the late eighteenth century was on the way to disappearing. The individual States in the United States, he said, were like the nobles in the Polish Republic. During the troubles in Poland, he observed, the nobles lived in affluence. At the same time, they were unwilling to sacrifice anything for their Republic which lacked the political and fiscal means to survive.[13] In

10. "Mémoire pour servir d'instructions au sieur marquis de Vergennes allant à Venise pour y résider en qualité d'ambassadeur de S.M.," 21 March 1779, printed in Pierre DuParc, ed., *Recueil des Instructions aux ambassadeurs et ministres de France* (Paris, 1958), 26:276.

11. The Dutch crisis of 1787 is described in Henry de Peyster, *Les Troubles de Hollande à la veille de la Révolution Francaise; 1780–1789* (Paris, 1905); Alfred Cobban, *Ambassadors and Secret Agents* (London, 1954); Jeremy Black, "The Marquis of Carmarthen and Relations with France, 1784–1789," *Francia* (West Germany) 12 (1985): 283–303. The European-wide nature of the crisis is developed in Black's "Sir Robert Ainslie: His Majesty's Agent-provocateur? British Foreign Policy and the International Crisis of 1787," *European History Quarterly* 14 (1984): 253–83; Simon Schama, *Patriots and Liberators: Revolution in the Netherlands, 1780–1813* (New York, 1977), 64–135.

12. Felix Gilbert, *To the Farewell Address: Ideas of Early American Foreign Policy* (Princeton, 1961), 99–100.

13. Otto to Vergennes, 9 April 1786, AAE-cp-EU, 31:208–14.

America, Otto continued, individuals and the States prospered and flourished, but the Congress and the Confederation floundered in permanent crisis.[14]

From the perspective of Versailles, it seemed that politics in a Republic too readily gave birth to "democracy" and "chaos." The two words meant almost the same thing to Louis XVI and he approved of neither. At one point in 1787, the French monarch even considered withdrawing his support to his allies, the Patriots, in the Dutch Republic because he thought they were too democratic.[15] In reports to Versailles, Otto spoke of the "absolute liberty" enjoyed by the people in America. The lower orders, he reported, seemed to want an "entire and unlimited" liberty, which could not exist except at the expense of public tranquillity.[16] In 1788, after almost eight months in the United States, the French minister Moustier also concluded that the weakness and ineptness of the Continental Congress was in part caused by the "phantom of democracy," which had seduced so many Americans. "The credulous majority was drunk with beautiful hopes."[17] The conduct of the United States, collectively and separately, Moustier reported, did little to confirm the idea of the superiority of a republican government.[18] Reflecting on the reports of democratic tendencies in the United States, Montmorin, Louis XVI's secretary of state for foreign affairs, noted that the tendencies seemed to be in every "province." The result, he predicted, could only be a weak confed-

14. On the notion that individuals and states prospered while the Confederacy floundered see Lawrence S. Kaplan, *Colonies into Nation*, 163. Kaplan writes: "But the triumphs of individual merchants and the durability of the economy were no tribute to the efficacy of the Confederation."

15. Pierre de Witt, *Une invasion prussienne en Hollande en 1787* (Paris, 1886), 186.

16. Otto to Vergennes, 20 September, 20 October 1786, AAE-cp-EU, 32:74, 88vo.

17. Moustier to Montmorin, 2 August 1788, ibid., 33:238.

18. Quoted in Cte. Renaud de Moustier, "Les État-Unis au lendemain de la guerre de l'independance," *Revue d'Histoire diplomatique* 6 (1892): 525.

eration.[19] It was a political picture that Otto and Moustier viewed with a mixture of curiosity and skepticism, that Montmorin, in Versailles, viewed with contempt, and Louis XVI viewed with horror.

The Confederation period was, indeed, a dangerous time for the Americans. They were seriously divided, not only over the question of what powers the central government should have, but also over issues of international relations. Spokesmen for western and southern interests in the United States vigorously protested what they feared to be a wholesale sell-out of their interests during the Jay-Gardoqui negotiations with Spain.[20] Westerners and Southerners had unsuccessfully demanded that Spain open the Mississippi to navigation. But the northeastern states were opposed. Representatives of the southern and western interests who approached Otto in the late summer of 1786 to see if they could persuade Louis XVI to support their position wanted Louis to provide his good offices in negotiations with Spain.[21]

By the spring of 1787, the inhabitants of Kentucky and the newly formed state of Franklin[22] were threatening to arm ten thousand men to settle the question of the navigation of the Mississippi for themselves. The opening of the Mississippi, Otto noted, would encourage the spread of the American population to the West,

19. Montmorin to Otto, 31 October 1787, AAE-cp-EU, 32:350.

20. Samuel Flagg Bemis, ed., *The American Secretaries of State and Their Diplomacy* (New York, 1927), 1:232–50; Lawrence S. Kaplan, *Colonies into Nation*, 168–73; Frederick W. Marks III, Independence on Trial: Foreign Affairs and the Making of the Constitution (Baton Rouge, 1973), 28.

21. Otto to Vergennes, 23 August, 10 September 1786, AAE-cp-EU, 32:58–60vo, 65.

22. The "lost" state of Franklin was formed in 1784 by the disgruntled inhabitants of present-day eastern Tennesee, after North Carolina ceded its western lands to the United States. Although Franklin adopted a permanent constitution in 1785, it was never recognized by the United States Continental Congress; in 1788 its territory reverted temporarily to North Carolina: see S. C. Williams, *History of the Lost State of Franklin* (1933).

which, in turn, would weaken the already overextended United States government.[23] Moreover, expansion threatened to provoke wars with the Indians. Indeed, by November of 1786, Otto wrote of the "alarming" reports of clashes with the Indians. Such wars, Otto believed, would be, "in the present exhaustion of finances [of the United States], one of the greatest of calamities."[24] The notion that the United States would grow and eventually clash with its neighbors seems, in this case, not based on a fear of the abuse of power by the Confederation, but rather on the fear that the Continental Congress would never have the means or authority to contain the rebellious individuals and expansionists bordering the Ohio and Mississippi Rivers.[25]

France's opposition to American expansion was interpreted by some of the founding fathers and many later historians as evidence that France not only abandoned the United States but became actively hostile after the Revolutionary War. Arthur Burr Darling probably expressed the most extreme judgment. The refusal of France to assist the Americans to expand he interpreted as hostility to the United States. Darling could read only "diplomatic verbiage"[26]

23. Otto to Vergennes, 5 March 1787, ibid., 32:207–16vo.

24. Otto to Vergennes, 10 September, 1 November 1786, ibid., 32:66vo, 123.

25. Henry E. Bourne, ed., "Correspondence of the Comte de Moustier with the Comte de Montmorin, 1787–1789," printed in *American Historical Review* 8 (1902–3): 713.

26. Arthur Burr Darling, *Our Rising Empire: 1763–1803* (New Haven, 1940), 117. Darling was also persuaded that Louis XVI secretly planned to restore the French empire in America by re-acquiring Louisiana. His opinion regarding France and Louisiana is, in part, based on a memoir written by Moustier entitled "A Memoire on the interesting question, often raised in America and sometimes in Europe: if it is appropriate for France to desire the retrocession of Louisiana" [Mémoire sur une question interessante, souvent agité en Amérique et quelquefois en Europe: s'il convient à la france de désirer la retrocession de la Louisiane], January 1789. AAE-cp-EU, Suppl. 6:169–330vo]. The memoir was not mailed until 10 March 1789. Moustier to Montmorin, 15 September 1789, AAE-cp-EU, 34:265. While this memoir is very interesting because of its descriptions of Americans, it had absolutely no discernible influence on Louis XVI's policies.

in Montmorin's reaction to the Spanish-American dispute over the opening of the Mississippi River to American shipping: while the Spanish might not understand their own interests very well, Montmorin opined, "that does not give the Americans the right to employ force against that power. The mouth of the Mississippi belongs to her [Spain]; she has therefore the right to open it or keep it closed, and the Americans can obtain special favors only by means of negotiation."[27]

French diplomats as well as officials in Versailles were acutely concerned about the expansionists ambitions of some Americans. Although Sweden, Austria, and Spain were long-term French allies and the Turks were long-time traditional friends, Louis XVI never assumed that an alliance with these powers obliged him to support them if they attacked their neighbors to expand their territory. And whenever they seemed to be preparing to do so, he vigorously opposed them. Moreover, France was not alone in its concern about American expansion. Great Britain, Spain, and native Americans all feared and tried to resist the territorial ambitions of the Americans.[28] The fact that they all failed does not mean that they did not clearly see the danger to their interests. Nor does it mean that their motives were hostile: tradition, international law, and public morality supported a state's right to its own territories. The maintenance of international stability was a fundamental principle in Louis XVI's foreign policy; aggressive expansion was a threat to stability.[29]

The fierce and volatile politics of the Confederation of the

27. Montmorin to Otto, 31 August 1787, AAE-cp-EU, 32:351.

28. Frederick W. Marks III, *Independence on Trial*, 19–23, 34–35.

29. French policy regarding expansion and Louis XVI's role as arbiter in the European balance of power system is outlined in "Mémoire de M. de Vergennes à Louis XVI sur la situation politique de la France relativement aux différentes puissances," 1774, K164, no. 2. Archives Nationales, and "Mémoire presenté au Roi par le Comte de Vergennes, 29 March 1784," AAE-md-France, 587:207–25; Orville T. Murphy, *Charles Gravier, Comte de Vergennes*, 211–21, 397–404, and passim.

United States made Louis XVI unwilling to intervene in American disputes. Furthermore, even if he had been tempted, the domestic and international crises in France and Europe would not have allowed him the luxury of doing so. By 1787, France was deeply involved in the conflict in the Dutch Republic. The exercise was proving difficult enough to deal with and that conflict was next door. Moreover, some of the American justifications for their demand for opening navigation on the Mississippi must have provoked disbelief at Versailles. A great river (so an inhabitant of Davidson County, North Carolina, told his representative in Congress) was a gift of Providence and could not be monopolized by any power.[30] In Europe, however, Providence had for centuries decreed otherwise. The powerful Emperor Joseph II himself did not enjoy free navigation on the Danube River, and the Dutch Republic had just recently successfully defended its right to keep the Scheldt River closed to navigation to the sea.

During the Scheldt River dispute, which did not end until 1785, Louis XVI risked his alliance with Joseph II to side with the Dutch in their refusal to open the river to navigation. Since the Peace of Westphalia in 1648, Europe had recognized the right of the Dutch to close the river. France was a guarantor of that peace, so to have supported the Americans' demand for opening the Mis-

---

30. "Traduction d'une lettre écrite par un habitant du Comté de Davidson dans la Caroline du Nord à un membre du Congres, Nashville le 20 October, 1786." Included with Montmorin to Otto, 31 August 1787, AAE-cp-EU, 32:212, 350–51; see also: "Resolution de la Législature de Virginie concernant la navigation du Mississippi du 29 November 1786," AAE-cp-Supplement, 6:325–26, which states: "Le droit de naviguer sur le Mississippi et de communiquer par ce canal avec d'autres nations doit être considéré comme un don, que la nature bienfaisante à fait aux Etats Unis comme souveraine du territoire orientale de ce fleuve et d'un grand nombre de rivières qui s'y jettent" [The right to navigate the Mississippi and to communicate by this channel with other nations ought to be considered as a gift, that a beneficent nature has given to the United States as the sovereign of the eastern territory of this river and of a great number of rivers which flow into it] (my translation).

sissippi would have involved pursuing a policy in America that contradicted a long-standing French policy in Europe.[31] Thus, what seemed a God-given right in North Carolina enjoyed little credence in Versailles and the rest of Europe. An attempt to mediate between Spain and the United States over the issue of the Mississippi River would surely have ended in embarrassment for Louis XVI. For these reasons, Moustier brought with him to New York, when he arrived as Louis XVI's minister in January of 1788,[32] instructions that included an unambiguous directive to stay out of the negotiations between the United States and Spain: " . . . the comte de Moustier will offer neither means of conciliation nor His Majesty's good offices." Intervention would only compromise France with all the interested parties.[33] The policy represented a radical departure from Louis's role as arbiter. Less than a year before he had lent his good offices to the negotiations between the United States and Algiers and Morocco.[34]

An additional source of concern for Versailles was that the peace settlement of 1783 did not establish harmony between the United States and Great Britain. The two countries were soon at loggerheads over violations and counterviolations of the peace treaty. As Versailles perceived the situation, there was no guarantee that the British army still on the American continent would remain inactive if the differences between the two nations were not settled peacefully or if a Franco-British conflict shattered the peace of Eu-

31. For the French rationale for Louis XVI's defense of the right of the Dutch to keep the Scheldt River closed: "Observations de M. de Vergennes sur le coup de canon tiré sur l'Escaut le 8 octobre, 1784," AAE-md-France, 1897:130.

32. Moustier's instructions are dated October 1787, but he did not arrive in the United States until January of 1788 after a long and difficult Atlantic voyage of 65 days, an ordeal that left him ill. "Instructions to Moustier, 10 October 1787," in Bourne, "Correspondence," 710–14; "LaLuzerne to Montmorin, 18 January 1788," AAE-cp-EU, 33:11.

33. "Instructions to Moustier," Bourne, "Correspondence," 710–14.

34. Vergennes to Otto, 25 August, 25 October 1786, AAE-cp-EU, 32:62vo, 117.

rope as it, indeed, threatened to do in 1787. For this reason, Louis kept a suspicious watch on the movements and activities of Englishmen in the United States.[35] Would Britain try to turn the unstable political situation in the United States to its advantage and destroy French influence there as she seemed, in fact, determined to do in the Dutch Republic? Otto expressed concern about this: "Britain is not indifferent to the confusion which reigns in every state except Connecticut. And if I am to believe several clever and knowledgeable persons, she still holds some hope of recovering a part of the United States." Personally, Otto did not believe the British ministry would "be so blind" as to try to take back any of the territory lost to the United States. The real aim of British agents in the United States, he thought, was to develop opportunities for Anglo-American trade.[36]

Because he sought a relaxation of tensions between Versailles and London after 1783, Louis XVI was careful to keep the issue of commerce between the United States and Great Britain from becoming a point of friction between France and Great Britain. When the comte d'Adhémar left Versailles to become France's ambassador to London, his orders were clear on this point: "It is natural," d'Adhémar's instructions read, "for the king [Louis XVI] to try to profit from a revolution that was his own work." On the other hand, the instruction continued, "it is in the interest of Great Britain not to lose the commerce of America." Furthermore, it was in Great Britain's interest to form with the United States political ties that could replace those broken by the Revolution. "This matter," d'Adhémar was told, "requires the greatest of vigilance." The ambassador was instructed, consequently, to keep a close watch on any projects the British government might develop regarding the United States. But if London inquired about the nature of the commercial relations between the United States and France, d'Ad-

35. Bourne, "Correspondence:" 711–14.
36. Otto to Vergennes, 16 March 1787, AAE-cp-EU, 32:222–223vo.

hémar was to refer them to the treaty of friendship and commerce France had signed with the Americans in 1778. If the British studied that treaty, d'Adhémar was told, they would find that Louis XVI had "left intact the perfect independence of the United States." That meant that Louis XVI had left the Americans "an entire liberty to form other political or mercantile ties." Louis XVI assured d'Adhémar that he was resolved to continue this policy. He would never consider it a violation of trust if the Americans decided to establish political or commercial relations with Great Britain.[37] The Confederation was weak and fragile, but it was a sovereign state and Louis XVI recognized it as such. At the same time, Louis XVI saw French commerce with the new American Republic as a way to attach the United States to France and to provide some ground of mutual interest that would allow French influence to be exerted in the United States. The Anglo-French Commercial Treaty of 1786 with Britain, the French commercial treaty with Sweden, and the Franco-Russian commercial treaty of 1787 had similar political aims.

By mid-1787 France was in deep financial trouble and preoccupied with its own diplomatic, political, and constitutional crises. Beyond the frontiers in the Dutch Republic, with the friends of France were under attack, there was a very real danger of a war that might involve France, Prussia and Great Britain, perhaps all of Europe. France's ally Sweden seemed determined to attack Russia. France's long-term interests in the Levant were increasingly undermined by Russia's obsession to expand at the expense of the Turks. Consequently, Louis XVI did not—could not—give full attention to Franco-American relations. Montmorin was fully aware that Americans were disappointed that France had not provided

---

37. The phrase is "qu'il [le Roi] ne fera jamais un crime aux Américains d'avoir des rapports avec la Grande Bretagne." "Mémoire pour servir d'instruction au sieur Comte d'"Adhémar . . . allant en Angleterre en Qualité d'Ambassadeur de la part de sa Majesté," in Paul Vaucher, ed., *Recueil des instructions aux ambassadeurs et ministres de France* (Paris, 1965), vol. XXV-2, tome 3, Angleterre, 517–19.

them with more trade advantages, especially in the French Caribbean islands. But Louis XVI's own domestic political problems did not leave him free to grant to the Americans concessions that would be prejudicial to the economic interests of his own subjects. While the doctrine of absolutism granted the king enormous theoretical authority, the political realities of 1786–89 demanded that Louis XVI recognize the enormous force of public opinion.[38]

In addition, there were so many obstacles to international commerce in the United States that Otto concluded that the commercial treaty between the United States and France could not remain intact.[39] The most notable obstacle to better trade relations was the weakness of the Continental Congress. The near impotence of that body made commercial treaties difficult to implement, because the Confederation had no power to enforce them.[40] "Does the present Congress," queried a French merchant in 1785, "have sufficient power to make a treaty on the basis of reciprocal advantages?"[41] "If the Congress dissolves or remains in the state of weakness in which it now exists," Moustier later warned, "I believe we shall be obliged to deal with each state individually." "It is impossible in the present circumstances to undertake anything with this absolutely inert body."[42] Furthermore, Moustier was convinced that

38. A measure of the fierce opposition of French commercial interests to Louis XVI's commercial policies is found in the reactions of the Chamber of Commerce of Rouen against the Anglo-French Commercial Treaty of 1786: Chambre du Commerce de Normandy, "Observations de la Chambre du Commerce de Normandie sur le Traité de Commerce entre la France et l'Angleterre" (Rouen, 1788); see also: Marie Donaghay, "The Exchange of Products of the Soil," 401; for discussion of the important role of public opinion in late eighteenth-century France, see Jack R. Censor and Jeremy D. Popkin, eds., *Press and Politics in Pre-Revolutionary France* (Berkeley, 1987), esp. vii–x; 208–24.

39. Otto to Vergennes, 10 February 1786, AAE-cp-EU, 31:83.

40. Frederick W. Marks III, *Independence on Trial*, 3.

41. "Queries Concerning Trade with the French Colonies, ca. December 1785," printed in Julian P. Boyd, ed., *The Papers of Thomas Jefferson*, 9:134–35.

42. Moustier to Montmorin, 21 April 1788, AAE-cp-EU, 33:164–64vo.

France was at a disadvantage negotiating its commercial interests with the United States. Congress could and did demand concessions, but it could promise absolutely nothing in return, because the government lacked the power to meet its commitments. It was in France's interest, Moustier argued, that the Americans abandon their present state of political indecision.[43]

News from the United States made it apparent that future Franco-American trade hinged on the outcome of the debate in Philadelphia over a new constitution. Some Americans, it appeared, were very much opposed to commercial relations with Europe. Moustier identified these Americans as "Anti-Federalists."[44] Europe, one vocal opponent of trade argued, could provide only luxury goods inappropriate to the simple lifestyle of a new nation.[45] That argument was not new to Versailles. Russians who had opposed the Franco-Russian trade agreement of 1787 expressed the same opinion. The Russian minister Voroncov sincerely believed that trade with France would "corrupt our [Russian] morals."[46] Thus, to Moustier, French trading interests, the Federalists and the new constitution were part of the same package.

After the peace of 1783, there were few mutual interests, other than trade, to hold the Franco-American alliance together. The Americans sharply limited their political involvement with Europe.[47] Accordingly, some of them, such as John Jay, even viewed

43. Ibid., 162–63vo.

44. Moustier to Montmorin, 25 June 1788, ibid., 214vo-15.

45. Ibid.; Otto to Vergennes, 20 September 1786, ibid., 32:73vo. Stephen Higginson, a wealthy Boston merchant, believed that the importation of *English* luxury goods undermined American frugality and high morals. "Letter of Stephen Higginson," *Annual Report of the American Historical Association for the Year 1896* 1 (Washington, 1897): 719.

46. Quoted in J. L. Regemorter, "Commerce et politique: préparation et négociation du traité Franco-Russe de 1787," *Cahiers du Monde Russe et Soviétique* 4 (1963): 246.

47. William C. Stinchcombe, *The American Revolution and the French Alliance* (Syracuse, 1969), 206–7.

the defense alliance of 1778 as having been terminated, once the peace treaty ended hostilities.[48] While France did not agree with that interpretation, it came as no surprise to Versailles. In fact, the year the peace treaty was signed, France's representative in the United States, La Luzerne, predicted that France and the United States would drift apart and the United States and Britain, because of their mutual interests in trade, would move closer together. When he read La Luzerne's observations, Vergennes apparently resigned himself to letting things "follow their natural movement."[49] Officially, however, he maintained the position that the "Treaty of February, 1778 . . . is not yet annulled."[50] Later, Vergennes's successor, Montmorin, expressed astonishment when he heard the opinion that the alliance was terminated. Furthermore, he reported, the king and his council were also "singularly astonished."[51] No matter how Louis XVI viewed the status of the 1778 treaty, he certainly did not consider all of France's relations with the United States terminated. Some political leaders in the United States also did not agree that there should be an end to Franco-American relations. Benjamin Franklin's earlier advice to Congress still carried weight: "We know not how soon we may have a fresh Occasion for Friends, for Credit, and for Reputation."[52]

After mid-1787, the clouds of war hanging over Europe and the death of Vergennes forced Montmorin to reevaluate all of France's alliances, including the Franco-American treaty. If the Dutch crisis erupted into another Franco-British war, what value would the alliance with the United States have for Louis XVI? Very little, Montmorin believed. France, he observed, had never intended to make of the United States a useful ally.[53] He recognized, further-

48. Ibid., 200.   49. Quoted in ibid. at 203.

50. Vergennes to Otto, 25 August 1786, AAE-cp-EU, 32:63vo.

51. Montmorin to Moustier, 23 June 1788, in Bourne, "Correspondence," 738.

52. Quoted in Stinchcombe, *The American Revolution*, 206.

53. Montmorin to Moustier, 31 October 1787, AAE-cp-EU, 32:350–350vo.

more, that in the event of an Franco-British war, the Continental Congress would incline toward neutrality. Louis XVI, Montmorin speculated, would probably consent to that disposition.[54] But Montmorin did not want that possibility broadcast as policy. He instructed the comte de Moustier, therefore, that "His Majesty attaches a great value to the maintenance of his alliance with the United States." He told Moustier to strengthen among the Americans the principles that would further unite them to France.[55] Early in 1789, Moustier proudly reported that he had succeeded in reestablishing in Congress the idea that the United States ought to regard the alliance as still in effect.[56]

After observing at first hand the ineffectiveness of the Continental Congress and realizing that it had only a "shadow" of sovereign power, Moustier concluded that "in the present situation the Congress cannot be of any use to the allies of the United States and is not even in a state to oppose its enemies." The Americans, he said, have no navy, no army, no fortifications, and the government had no coercive power to undertake to build them. "I believe," he wrote to Montmorin, "that the present form of Government cannot possibly continue."[57] Moustier was repeating what Otto had already observed: the United States was too weak to fulfill any diplomatic engagements to France.[58]

An ally so weak it was paralyzed was of no use to France. More importantly, it could easily become a victim of the aggression of others, especially in the dangerous international world of 1787. In Philadelphia, some of the delegates debating the new Constitution agreed. If a government, Federalists argued, could not become respectable, it could not remain neutral.[59] Moustier's dispatches to

54. Ibid., 370vo.   55. Bourne, "Correspondence," 710.

56. Moustier to Montmorin, 19 January 1789, AAE-cp-EU, 34:8.

57. Moustier to Montmorin, 8 Febuary 1788, ibid., 33:16–21vo.

58. Otto to Vergennes, 20 September 1786, ibid., 32:75.

59. For an extended discussion of how the Federalists and the Antifederalists viewed foreign policy under the Confederation see: Frederick W. Marks III, *Independence on Trial*; Lawrence S. Kaplan, *Colonies into Nation*.

Versailles, as well as those of his predecessor, repeatedly stressed that the Continental Congress had, indeed, reached paralysis. Moustier feared that if the Dutch crisis spawned a new Franco-British war, the British might take advantage of the weakness of the United States and attempt to take back the major United States seaports in order to control American commerce. American military capacities were so limited that the United States would not be able to defend itself. If such a threat appeared imminent, Moustier advised, France must send its own naval squadrons to occupy the important ports. France could guarantee evacuation after the war.[60]

Louis XVI had other reasons to want a strong and stable United States government. His own debts, deficits, and near bankruptcy made him especially conscious about debt payments. The United States had agreed to begin payments in 1786 on the loans it had contracted with France during the War.[61] But Otto saw no hope whatsoever that the United States could pay back on schedule the money owed Louis XVI. All demands for payment, he reported, were useless.[62] Persuaded, Montmorin concluded that France had little chance of soon recovering that money. Louis XVI did not give up asking for payment, however. If not payment on the principals of the loans, he wanted, at least, payment of interests.[63]

It was clear to the French representatives in America that if

60. Moustier to Montmorin, 10 February 1788, AAE-cp-EU, 33:22–26vo.

61. The interest on the 1783 French loan to the United States was to begin January 1785. "Etat des avances paites par le Roi au Congrès des Etats-Unis de l'Amérique pendant la dernière guerre et des époques auxquelles le Congrès s'est engagé à rembourser les Capitaux et Interêts . . ." AAE-Comptabilité, Finances du Ministère, 6:376. See also the two contracts in Charles I. Bevan, ed., "Contract between the King and the Thirteen United States of North America," 16 July 1782 and 25 February 1783, *Treaties and Other International Agreements of the United States of America, 1779–1949* (Washington, D.C., 1971), 16 July 1782: Art. 2, 785; 25 February 1783: Art. 4, 790.

62. Otto to Montmorin, 19 May 1787, AAE-cp-EU, 32:262vo–263.

63. Bourne, "Correspondence," 712–13.

France was ever to receive payment on the loans made to the United States, the American government would have to be strong enough to levy and collect taxes. But the Continental Congress, in fact, lacked effective taxing-power to raise money.[64] It needed more authority to "take its share" from "the citizen's pocket."[65] Furthermore, if the United States split apart as a result of the weakness of its government, it was even less likely to pay back its loans. In any case, Americans were too absorbed in their own constitutional crisis, Moustier concluded, to see the urgency of France's financial problems. He suggested a dramatic way France might get their attention. The British, he noted, were still occupying certain military posts in the United States until the Americans paid debts owed British subjects. When Elizabeth was queen of Britain, he recalled, she ordered troops to occupy places in the Dutch Republic until the Dutch paid what they owed her. If Congress did not soon do something to meet its commitments to France, Moustier suggested, France might follow the British example.[66]

There is no evidence that anyone in Versailles seriously considered implementing Moustier's suggestion to occupy the ports of the United States to force the payment of debts. By 1788, when the suggestion was made, France's financial resources were so exhausted that she had even abandoned her allies in the Dutch Republic. But Otto's and Moustier's briefs for the idea that the extraordinary weakness and instability of the United States government was not in France's interest did have some effect. By degrees, Montmorin moved closer to the opinions of his diplomats. In June of 1788, the secretary of state for foreign affairs was of the opinion that if the new Constitution were not adopted, the United States would become a "phantom." And France "would be forced to negotiate its interests with each particular state." However, if the

64. Frederick W. Marks III, *Independence on Trial*, 33–34; William Stinchecombe, *The American Revolution*, 210–11.
65. Otto to Vergennes, 25 October 1786, AAE-cp-EU, 32:117vo.
66. Moustier to Montmorin, 25 June 1788, AAE-cp-EU, 33:215vo–16vo.

Constitution were adopted, he concluded, the United States would acquire "force and energy." He told Moustier, therefore, that while he was still officially to abstain from taking sides or intervening in the debates over the new Constitution, he was free to say that Louis XVI would look with satisfaction on changes that would "assure and consolidate the political existence, the tranquillity and the happiness of the United States." Moreover, Moustier was told to make it clear to the Americans that Louis XVI's reluctance to take sides in the internal affairs of the United States was not a sign that he did not care about the fate of the new nation. Louis' official neutrality was an "homage" to American independence; it was not evidence of indifference.[67] As the crisis in France edged toward revolution, Louis XVI necessarily turned to other matters. Moustier, however, continued to plead with Montmorin to do more to show the Americans they had France's support. Louis XVI's "indifference" to the developments in the United States, he warned, would inevitably become a source of the "most alarming evils," evils that would inevitably condition future diplomatic relations between the two powers.[68]

By the fall of 1789 the crisis in the United States had begun to calm. A new Congress made up of men Moustier called "the most distinguished" had assembled and seemed to have won public support. As Otto earlier predicted, a strong American government under a new constitution was more able to pay its debts. In September, Moustier met with Alexander Hamilton, the United States secretary of the treasury, who outlined for the French minister his plan to borrow money in Holland to begin paying the foreign debts of the United States. The United States Senate had recently ratified a Franco-American consular convention to facilitate trade. George Washington, a man thoroughly trusted at Versailles, became president. Thomas Jefferson had replaced John Jay as head

67. Montmorin to Moustier, 23 June 1788, ibid., 208–9.
68. Moustier to Montmorin, 25 December 1788, ibid., 385.

of the Department of Foreign Affairs. These events set the stage for a different kind of relation between France and the United States and augured well for the future.

Unfortunately, Louis XVI could no longer effectively respond to the new situation. His inability to defend his own nation's interests in Europe was now a public scandal. Frustrated by opposition and defeat at home, he watched his government grind to a halt in the face of debts, vicious public criticism, lack of political support, and violence.[69] Time was running out for the French monarchy. Within months, the opportunity for Louis XVI to develop a different and perhaps more solid partnership with a stable United States government vanished altogether.

In summary, the descriptions of the United States Confederation pictured in Otto's and Moustier's dispatches clearly indicate that they believed that the union formed by the articles of Confederation of the United States was weak, disintegrating and unable to perform in the international arena.[70] Their perceptions of American politics and government support the conclusion that "the weaknesses of the Articles of Confederation showed up more clearly in the area of foreign policy."[71]

It is equally clear that French diplomats saw the weakness of the Confederation in foreign affairs to be a serious threat to France's interests. It was not in France's interest if Congress's power to collect taxes withered to the point where the United States could not meet the obligations of its foreign debts. If the central government lost to the states all control over international trade, France would find it cumbersome to negotiate commercial agreements with each state. Only a strong United States government could restrain the

69. Cte Renaud de Moustier, "Les Etats-Unis au Lendemain," 203.

70. Obviously the French diplomats would not have agreed with Merrill Jensen's conclusion that such a picture of the Confederation is "at worst false and at best grossly distorted" (*The New Nation; A History of the United States during the Confederation: 1781–1789* [New York, 1962], xiii).

71. Paul A. Varg, *Foreign Policies of the Founding Fathers* (Baltimore, 1970), 50.

expansionist ambitions of Americans who threatened the interests of Spain, Great Britain, the native Americans as well as France. If the United States remained so weak that it was a temptation to the British army or navy in a general European war, France could not view the situation with indifference. Independence of the United States was one of the fundamental aims of the War of the American Revolution. And after the war Louis XVI—with a good deal of self-satisfaction—made it clear to the British that France had not abandoned that policy. But to French diplomats observing the Confederation, the establishment of independence required more on the part of the Americans than the signing of the peace treaty of 1783. It is a cruel irony of history that, by 1789, weaknesses of the central government, the specter of debts and bankruptcy, and international impotence, once perceived as American problems, were now Louis XVI's own problems.

EIGHT

War

THE WAR the French representative at Constantinople feared at the beginning of 1787 came before the year ended. It was not a surprise, but the abrupt manner of its beginnings startled Versailles and left Louis XVI's ambassador confused about how to respond. As 1787 opened, Bulgakow, the Russian ambassador at Constantinople, suddenly and without any warning demanded a renegotiation of all the issues that the Turks and the Russians, with French mediation, were on the verge of settling. Every question was now back on the table for renegotiation. The Turks, puzzled by the sudden about-face, concluded that the Russians had used the long negotiations to prepare secretly an attack on the Ottoman Empire. Had they been led into a trap, asked the Turks, a trap set by Bulgakow and assisted by the French mediator?[1] Turkish suspicions were so deep and Turkish officials so hostile that the French ambassador and mediator, Choiseul-Gouffier, found it difficult to find anyone who would listen to his explanation of France's motives.[2] Nevertheless, when the Turks began rearming in response to the new Russian attitude, they again turned to Louis XVI for military equipment and engineers to help them put their fortifications in order.[3]

1. Choiseul-Gouffier to Vergennes, 25 January 1787, AAE-cp-Turquie, 175:36–48.
2. Ibid., 175:48vo.
3. Choiseul-Gouffier to Vergennes, 10 February 1787, ibid., 175:54vo.

Perplexed by the unexpected change in Russian behavior, the French ambassador nevertheless offered French mediation once again. He even suggested, at the risk of adding fuel to the outrage of the Turks, that they consider making additional concessions to the Russians in order to avoid war. But in truth, he did not know what to do, so he sent a courier posthaste to Versailles to ask for instructions. He needed immediate advice about the role of the French military advisers in the Ottoman Empire. Should he allow the French army engineers there make repairs on the Turkish fortress at Oczakow? He knew, of course, that if the Russians took Oczakow in a war, any French soldiers captured there would be a major embarrassment to Louis XVI.

At Versailles, the report of Bulgakow's new posture was an unexpected and frustrating disappointment. Patient French mediation had produced the settlement the Russians now seemed determined to destroy. While Louis XVI did not care how most of the topics reopened for discussion were settled, the new Russian reversal compromised him as mediator. Versailles recognized that Russia and the Turks were on a collision course.[4] The Turks interpreted the Russian demands as deliberate insults to the sultan and to the Muslim religion.[5] War now appeared inevitable, although it would still be several months before it began. Meanwhile, the Turks were not prepared and France, faced with the obvious threats to its influence and interests in the Ottoman Empire, seemed unable to respond effectively.

If war broke out, France certainly could not create a diversion useful to the Turks without the help of either Britain, Austria, or Prussia. Versailles had no idea how Louis XVI's *and* Catherine's ally, Austria, would react. Austria needed to keep her alliance with Russia as a counterweight to Prussia. Nevertheless, the Hapsburgs realized that if they did not limit Russian expansion, they would

4. "Lu au Conseil d'Etat le Mardi, 28 February 1787," ibid., 175:90–93.
5. Ibid., 175:90–93.

eventually have the formidable Russian army rather than the weak Turkish army on their borders.[6] At the same time, France could not hope for assistance from Britain or Prussia, because at that very moment French relations with the two powers were deteriorating over the volatile situation in the Dutch Republic. Finally, to "these difficulties," concluded the brief read in the king's council, was added the most pressing issue of all, the "embarrassment of our finances."[7] Meanwhile, the Turks began to look elsewhere for diplomatic and military support.[8]

Choiseul-Gouffier's dispatches continued to bring bad news. While the Turkish government seemed, momentarily, more circumspect, the Turkish minister who had earlier accepted French mediation was dismissed, exiled, and replaced by a religious fanatic. Members of the Turkish government showed no restraint in expressing their resentments and distrust of France.[9] The Turkish government suffered from an "inconceivable anarchy" and if the Russians attacked Oczakow by sea, Choiseul-Gouffier predicted, the place would fall within hours.[10] Aware of the deplorable state of Turkish military preparations, Montmorin told Choiseul-Gouffier to go ahead and use the French officers in the Ottoman Empire to repair and reinforce the fortifications at Oczakow, despite the very real risk of an encounter with Russia.[11] The summer of 1787 brought no relaxation of tensions. At St. Petersburg, the Russian ministry moderated its position and even began to dis-

6. Karl A. Roider, Jr., *Austria's Eastern Question: 1700–1790* (Princeton, 1982), 175.

7. "Lu au Conseil le Mardi, 28 Fevrier, 1787," ibid., AAE-cp-Turquie, 175:90–93.

8. Montmorin to Ségur, 15 March 1787, AAE-cp-Russie, 120:139–140; Montmorin to Choiseul-Gouffier, 7 August 1788, AAE-cp-Turquie, 178:9–12.

9. Choiseul-Gouffier to Vergennes, 25 January 1787, ibid., 175:55; Choiseul-Gouffier to Montmorin, 24 March 1787, ibid., 175:138.

10. Choiseul-Gouffier to Montmorin, 24 March 1787, ibid., 175:141–43.

11. Montmorin to Choiseul-Gouffier, 29 March, 26 April 1787, ibid., 175:155–61, 230–32.

tance itself from Bulgakow's brusque actions.[12] But by July it was clear that the Turkish grand vizir had decided to go to war. Choiseul-Gouffier believed the grand vizir was being encouraged secretly by the British ambassador to declare war.[13] The Turks, on the other hand, were convinced that the Russians were set to launch an attack on them.[14]

Choiseul-Gouffier now fully expected war.[15] Nevertheless, long after the war actually began, Versailles continued to instruct him to bring Bulgakow and the Turks back to the negotiating table.[16] Louis XVI acted on the slim hope that although Russia's Bulgakow had put the crisis in motion, Catherine was now declaring her "pacific sentiments."[17] But the Turks no longer listened to offers of French mediation. With a perverse mixture of official fatalism and ritual solemnity, they plunged into war.[18] Choiseul-Gouffier could only deplore the decision. The sultan, he bemoaned, had completely lost control of his military and his government. The French ambassador was convinced that peace had been within easy reach of both powers. But neither side sincerely wanted it.[19]

The Turks, provoked by Bulgakow's behavior into the role of aggressors, faced a difficult war. Catherine could now ask Joseph II for the assistance stipulated in their alliance.[20] The consequences of such a request, Montmorin feared, could be immense: "There is no court in Europe which can be certain that it is not going to be involved."[21] Furthermore, Versailles knew that Oczakow would likely

12. Choiseul-Gouffier to Montmorin, 25 May 1787, ibid., 175:275.

13. Choiseul-Gouffier to Montmorin, 24 July 1787, ibid., 176:51ff.

14. Choiseul-Gouffier to Montmorin, 3 August 1787, ibid., 176:69–79, 84–92.

15. Choiseul-Gouffier to Montmorin, 9 August 1787, ibid., 176:88.

16. Montmorin to Choiseul-Gouffier, 2 October 1787, ibid., 176:230–31vo.

17. Ibid.

18. Choiseul-Gouffier to Montmorin, 16 August 1787, ibid., 176:111–13.

19. Choiseul-Gouffier to Montmorin, 9 August 1787, ibid., 176:88–89.

20. Montmorin to Choiseul-Gouffier, 2, 21 October, 25 November 1787, ibid., 176:232–33vo, 268–69vo, 313–16.

21. Montmorin to Choiseul-Gouffier, 23 September 1787, ibid., 176:206.

fall to a Russian siege, and the French officers assisting in the defense preparations there would be captured. Louis XVI would have to explain himself to his new friends in St. Petersburg. Meanwhile, the Turks continued to test the limits of French patience by asking Louis XVI to provide them with ships to carry on the war. The request posed difficulties, given Louis XVI's determination to avoid doing anything to harm the new relations with Russia. Nevertheless, if he did not consent, he would likely destroy what little confidence the Turkish government still had in France.[22]

The Turkish request provided Choiseul-Gouffier with the chance to raise with the sultan an issue of great importance to France. The negotiations for the Franco-Russian commercial alliance nourished hopes that France might exploit the commercial opportunities of the Black Sea trade.[23] The Turks, however, were extremely reluctant to grant anyone the right to enter the Black Sea, a right France had "vainly solicited for twelve years."[24] Every time Choiseul-Gouffier requested of the sultan the permission to send French ships into the area to trade, he was refused.[25] Versailles repeatedly threatened to bring the French ambassador home, or even to withdraw French military advisers, if the Turks did not show more flexibility on the issue.[26] But the sultan would not budge.

The French naval buildup after the War of the American Revolution made entrance to the Black Sea of special urgency. To construct and repair the ships of its new navy, France purchased sizable amounts of wood from Russia. Shipped from the Dnieper through the Black Sea to the Mediterranean, the wood was des-

22. Choiseul-Gouffier to Montmorin, 25 September 1787, ibid., 176:217–18.

23. Montmorin to Choiseul-Gouffier, 28 May 1787, ibid., 175:280.

24. Choiseul-Gouffier to Montmorin, 24 March 1787, ibid., 175:138.

25. Choiseul-Gouffier to Montmorin, 24 July 1787, ibid., 176:51.

26. Vergennes to Choiseul-Gouffier, 11 January 1787, ibid., 175:10vo–11vo; Choiseul-Gouffier to Montmorin, 24 March 1787, ibid., 175:141–141vo; Choiseul-Gouffier to Montmorin, 24 July 1787, ibid., 176:54–55vo.

tined for the arsenal at Toulon. In 1781 the French government had provided extensive credit to a French merchant living in Constantinople to buy and ship to France masts and other naval stores in such abundant supply in Russia as well as Poland.[27] But as hostilities between Russia and the Ottoman Empire became almost certain during the summer of 1787, the Turks refused to permit passage of Russian ships through the Black Sea. In addition, the Russian flag was not respected by the Barbary pirates in the Mediterranean, creating concern that the much-needed wood would never reach France. For Louis XVI the answer was to ship the wood in French vessels. Press the Turks, Montmorin told the French ambassador. And if they refused France the right to enter the Black Sea, Choiseul-Gouffier was to warn them that Louis XVI might seek his interests in "other combinations."[28] "Other combinations," of course, meant closer relations with Russia.

The needs of war eventually provided a temporary solution to the shipping problem. Probably at the suggestion of the Turks, Choiseul-Gouffier recommended that Louis XVI offer the Turkish government the use of French ships to carry supplies. Montmorin quickly seized upon the idea and gave French sea captains permission to enter the Black Sea carrying Turkish goods. They were to avoid carrying goods, however, that violated any treaties France had signed. And they were especially warned not to sail to Oczakow, since it was under siege by the Russians and France did not want to risk a skirmish with the Russian navy. Otherwise, Montmorin said (perhaps with a hint of irony?), the idea was altogether consistent with the principles of Catherine's famous armed neutrality policy.[29] The idea had an additional virtue. The precedent of entering the Black Sea during the war, Montmorin hoped,

27. Paul Bamford, *Forests and French Sea Power* (Toronto, 1956), 195–203.

28. Montmorin to Choiseul-Gouffier, 23 April, 31 July, 22 August 1787, ibid., 175:146–146vo; 176:67, 138vo–39.

29. Montmorin to Choiseul-Gouffier, 6 September 1788, ibid., 178:79.

could serve as the basis for an article in the eventual Russo-Turkish peace treaty granting France the formal right to enter. Since France expected to be a mediator of the Russo-Turkish treaty of peace whenever it was signed, it seemed reasonable to hope it could include such an article in the final treaty.[30] Needless to say, the French Revolution extinguished all hope for that French mediation.

The Russo-Turkish war reminded Europeans that if the "Eastern Question" was not settled by diplomatic agreement among the interested powers, Catherine would settle it on her own terms. Those terms meant conquests and annexations, perhaps all the way to Constantinople. In Vienna, Catherine's aggressiveness caused mixed emotions. If the Turkish pie was to be cut, it seemed reasonable that Austria must have its share.[31] But as long as she lived, the empress of Austria, Maria Teresa, resisted Austrian participation in a partition of the Ottoman Empire for moral as well as economic reasons. The territory the Austrian Empire was likely to get from partition was poor and unproductive, full of the "wildest people" and likely to cost more to develop than it was worth. Furthermore, any Austrian agreement to partition the Turkish Balkan territories brought closer the day when Austria would have Russia at her doorstep.[32]

Louis XVI's firm stand against the partition of the Ottoman Empire was the legacy of his minister, the comte de Vergennes. But even Vergennes, on occasion, seemed suspiciously curious as to what might be France's compensation if a partition did take place.[33] Vergennes's successor, Montmorin, continued the legacy,

30. See the note: Montmorin to LaLuzerne, 16 June 1788, ibid., 177:236.

31. Karl A. Roider, *Austria's Eastern Question: 1700–1790* (Princeton, 1982), 132.

32. For an excellent discussion of Austria's responses to the Ottoman Empire see ibid., 132–50; 169–88; 191–96.

33. Orville T. Murphy, *Charles Gravier, Comte de Vergennes: French Diplomacy in the Age of Revolution, 1710–1787* (Albany, N.Y., 1982), 337–44.

but found it more and more difficult to support. The almost total collapse of French influence in Constantinople and the growing reality of unfettered Russian expansion into the Ottoman Empire demanded a reconsideration of policy. The implications of Russian expansion for French commerce in the Levant, as well as French recognition that a close Russian-French alliance might possibly exercise considerable influence in Europe, led Montmorin to consider the possibility of some kind of understanding with Catherine II. He wanted something that would protect, perhaps even expand, French commerce and include some territorial compensation for France if the Ottoman Empire should collapse. But to Montmorin this alternative was a measure of last resort; a way out of the "no-win" situation in which France found itself in the Ottoman Empire. Others in Louis XVI's government wanted more and were less patient. Anticipating the foreign policies of Napoleon, they favored partition of the Ottoman Empire, with France receiving Egypt.[34]

The Russian war with the Ottoman Empire was a silver hook dropped before the eyes of Gustavus III of Sweden. Immediately he arranged an unannounced visit to Denmark to get the support of that government for a war against Russia.[35] The Danish prince royal and his family were, in fact, his relatives.[36] Gustavus hoped to negotiate an alliance and use the opportunity of Russia's preoccupation with the war with the Turks to attack her in the north. But

34. For discussions of France's interests in the Ottoman Empire, especially its commercial interests, see: François Charles-Roux, "La politique française en Egypte à la fin du XVIIIe siècle," *Revue historique* 92 (1906): 1–20; 225–52. See also: Orville T. Murphy, "Napoleon's International Politics: How Much Did He Owe to the Past?" *Journal of Military Policy* 54, no. 2 (April 1990), 163–71.

35. LaHouze to Montmorin, 30 October 1787, AAE-cp-Dannemark, 166:109–13.

36. The Countess of Minto, *A Memoir of the Right Honorable Hugh Elliot* (Edinburgh, 1868), 301–2.

Denmark disappointed him.[37] He was, apparently, unaware that the Danes were already obliged by treaty to come to Russia's aid if it were attacked. He returned home empty-handed, but not perceptibly wiser.[38]

By the spring of 1788, Louis XVI suspected that Gustavus secretly planned an attack on Russia. While in Denmark, the Swedish monarch had boasted that, even if the rest of Europe chose to do nothing in the face of the Russo-Turkish war, he was not going to remain a "lazy spectator."[39] Fearful that Gustavus's reckless ambitions might embarrass France and create problems with Russia with whom France had just signed a commercial treaty, Montmorin instructed Louis XVI's minister at Stockholm to communicate to Gustavus how seriously an attack on Russia would damage Franco-Swedish relations. If Gustavus carried out his schemes, Louis XVI warned, the king of France could no longer regard him as anything but "an old friend who had failed him."[40]

Nevertheless, without an alliance with Denmark and with the support of France uncertain at best, Gustavus steadfastly pursued his project. Catherine II had decided to send a fleet from the Baltic to the Mediterranean to force the Dardenelles and attack the Turks as she had done in 1770, when her fleet destroyed the Ottoman fleet in the harbor at Cesme. When diplomats learned that Gustavus III was rearming his navy, they concluded that he was going

37. LaHouze to Montmorin, 11 December 1787, 5 February 1788, AAE-cp-Dannemark, 166:139–139vo.; 163–64.

38. Minto, *Memoir*, 303.

39. LaHouze to Montmorin, 22 April 1788, AAE-cp-Dannemark, 166:231–231vo.

40. A. Geffroy, *Gustave III et la Cour de France*, (Paris, 1867), 2:65–66; "Memoire pour servir de supplement aux instructions du Marquis de Pons, ambassadeur du Roi en Suède, retournant à Stockholm. 20 June, 1788," printed in A. Geffroy, ed., *Recueil des Instructions données aux ambassadeurs et ministres de France*, Suède, 476; LaHouze to Montmorin, 22 April 1788, AAE-cp-Dannemark, 166:231–231vo.

to intercept the Russian fleet and prevent it from reaching the Mediterranean. Suspicions were confirmed when the French ambassador to Copenhagen discovered that wagon loads of an estimated 18,000,000 livres in silver bars and specie packed in barrels were shipped to Sweden out of Hamburg. Such a sum of money was circumstantial evidence that Gustavus was about to undertake a very costly project. Once alerted, Versailles was predictably curious. Who supplied the money? French representatives at Copenhagen and Stockholm inquired everywhere among their informants, but found no answer. At first, they speculated that the British had subsidized Gustavus. Later, they decided it was the Turks. Actually, Montmorin discovered later that Gustavus had negotiated a huge loan on the Amsterdam money market.[41]

Gustavus did not wish to appear to be the aggressor in a war with Russia. His treaty with France stipulated aid only if he was attacked. Consequently, his ambassador to Versailles assured Montmorin that Sweden's rearmament and troop movements were only "defensive measures."[42] Nevertheless, in July of 1788 he used a random exchange of gunfire on the Finnish border as the pretext to claim he had been attacked. He opened the campaign with a quick Swedish naval victory at Hogland and a harsh ultimatum to Catherine II. The empress of Russia, Gustavus demanded, must punish her ambassador at Stockholm for improperly meddling in Swedish affairs; she must restore parts of Finland ceded to Russia in earlier treaties; and she must make, with Swedish mediation, a peace with the sultan of the Ottoman Empire.[43] Gustavus never

41. Gaussen to Montmorin, 11, 25 July 1788, AAE-cp-Suède, 281:35vo, 64; Pons to Montmorin, 29 July, 5 August 1788, ibid., 281:73, 101–101vo; Montmorin to Gaussens, 17 August 1788, ibid., 281:131; LaHouze to Montmorin, 6, 13 May, 10, 17 June, 1788, AAE-cp-Dannemark, 166:239–40; 241; 256–57vo; 259–60vo. Also, La-Houze to Montmorin, 2 September 1788, ibid., 354vo.

42. Montmorin to Gaussen, 6 July 1788, AAE-cp-Suède, 281:16–17.

43. Geffroy, *Gustave III et la Cour de France* , 68–69.

attacked the Russian fleet destined for the Mediterranean, but his military action forced Catherine to cancel its sailing orders in order to keep her naval forces in the Baltic. Whatever else Gustavus had accomplished, he performed a valuable service for the sultan. Next, he asked France for the aid stipulated in his secret treaty with Louis XVI.

Gustavus's actions confounded Versailles. All during the spring and summer buildup of Swedish armaments, Louis XVI had repeatedly warned him against starting a war with Russia. No matter what resources Gustavus had at his disposal, the French told Gustavus, he could never match those at the disposal of Catherine.[44] But a war on Russia obsessed Gustavus. And when he designed and executed his plans, he did so without consulting or even informing his ally Louis XVI. Moreover, the war in the Baltic meant that the recent agreement to allow French shipping to use the Swedish entrepôt at Göteborg was rendered worthless. Louis XVI sent ambassador Pons, who was in France on leave, posthaste back to Stockholm with orders to inform Gustavus that Louis XVI would not provide aid because Gustavus had not been attacked. Louis agreed, however, to fulfill the conditions of the treaty that required that he offer his good offices.[45]

The diplomatic momentum of Gustavus's naval victory and extravagant demands quickly decelerated when his army officers at the front mutinied, protesting that his aggression against Catherine violated the Swedish constitution. The revolt was so serious that Pons later called it a "revolution." "[Gustavus's] blow [against Catherine II] has failed," he wrote to Versailles, "and today this Prince is in the greatest of embarrassment."[46] Embarrassment in-

44. Gaussens to Montmorin, 11 July 1788, AAE-cp-Suède, 281:31–34vo.

45. Montmorin to Gaussen, 6, 31 July 1788, ibid., 281:16–18vo, 81–84.

46. Pons to Montmorin, 8, 19, 27 August 1788, ibid., 281:121–27vo, 139–40vo, 157–58vo ; LaHouze to Montmorin, 5, 19 August 1788, AAE-cp-Dannemark, 166:316vo, 336–41.

deed! The Danes met the engagements stipulated in their treaty with Catherine, and a Danish army under Prince Charles of Hesse invaded Sweden with 12,000 men.[47] At Stockholm, the Swedish Senate seized the opportunity to try to recover some of the authority it had lost to Gustavus in the coup of 1772. Gustavus stood at the very edge of a military and political catastrophe.[48]

As they watched the drama unfold in the north, the ministries of Europe grew alarmed. In France, Louis XVI did not want to abandon Gustavus, but he also did not want and could not afford a war in the north. Furthermore, France's newly formed, but still fragile, relations with Russia could not possibly survive a war in which France supported Sweden. He ordered his ambassador to St. Petersburg to open discussions with Catherine to explore whether or not she would agree to a hasty peace with Gustavus.[49] Britain, too, shared the alarm. George III was not always on friendly terms with Sweden, but he did not want to see Swedish power destroyed, and that scenario seemed possible, since France, Sweden's ally, appeared unable to help. If Sweden collapsed, Russia would surely dominate the Baltic. The British government communicated its alarm in a general way to Hugh Elliot, its minister in Copenhagen, because Britain had no representative in Stockholm.[50]

Elliot reacted with characteristic flair. He asked Copenhagen to support his plan for a reconciliation between Russia and Sweden. But Denmark refused on the grounds of her treaty obligations to Catherine.[51] Consequently, Elliot set out for Sweden. Once again he explained to London: "The pressing circumstances of His

47. LaHouze to Montmorin, 7 October 1788, ibid., 166:382.
48. Pons to Montmorin, 26 August 1788, AAE-cp-Suède, 281:152–56vo; La-Houze to Montmorin, 2 September 1788, AAE-cp-Dannemark, 166:352–352vo.
49. Montmorin to Pons 4 September 1788, AAE-cp-Suède, 281:171–73vo; Montmorin to LaHouze 13 July 1788, AAE-cp-Dannemark, 166:299vo.
50. Minto, *Memoir*, 305.
51. LaHouze to Montmorin, 2 September 1788, AAE-cp-Dannemark, 166:353–54.

Swedish Majesty and the immediate danger to which the balance of the North was exposed, left me no time to wait for further instructions than those [general instructions] contained in your lordship's dispatches."[52] Before leaving Copenhagen, Elliot knew (having received news from Berlin) that Prussia also saw the very real danger of a Swedish collapse in the Baltic. Frederick William II was prepared to second British attempts to mediate the conflict. Confident that Russia was too deeply involved in the Turkish war to stop him, Frederick William II announced he would march Prussian troops into Danish Holstein if Prince Charles of Hesse did not withdraw his troops from Swedish territory.[53]

It was a classic chess move of eighteenth-century diplomacy, and for both the British and the Prussians the move provided the additional sweet satisfaction of exposing the impotence of France. Louis XVI was unable to provide military assistance or effective diplomatic support to his ally. And although he offered his good offices to advance the peace, he did not immediately offer to mediate. Soon the Dutch joined the British and Prussians and all three stepped forward to support Gustavus, who was desperate and searching everywhere for help.[54] The British, Prussian and Dutch diplomats, seized the initiative. Elliot's melodramatic version of what happened in Sweden speaks for itself:[55]

On my arrival in Sweden, after a search of eleven days I traced the King [Gustavus] wandering from place to place, endeavoring to animate his unarmed peasants to hopeless resistance. His very couriers were ignorant of his abode. At length, exhausted with fatigue and illness, I reached the King at Carlstadt, upon the 29th of September. Here I found his carriage ready to convey him to a place of greater security; without generals, without troops, and with few attendants, he was devoid of every means of de-

52. Minto, *Memoir*, 305.

53. Ibid., 305–6; LaHouze to Montmorin, 28 October 1788, AAE-cp-Dannemark, 166:412.

54. Montmorin to Pons, 25 September 1788, AAE-cp-Suède, 281:216–19vo.

55. Minto, *Memoir*, 306–7.

fense. . . . He was on the point of falling victim to the ambition of Russia, the treachery of Denmark, and the factious treason of his nobility. In the sincerity of distress the King also added, "to the mistakes of his own conduct."

Elliot explained to Gustavus that the British and Prussian governments were prepared to help him. Gustavus was overjoyed, especially when he learned that Prussia stood behind him against Danish or Russian attempts to change the Swedish constitution to help the nobles recover some of their lost power.[56] "On further explanation," Elliot reported, "the King consented to adopt all those measures which I thought most suitable to his situation." Next Elliot began to organize Swedish defenses; once again he called upon the British seamen then in Swedish harbors to help man batteries.[57] He then found the headquarters of Prince Charles of Hesse and he warned him that Denmark ran the risk of a break with Britain and Prussia if the invasion continued. Faced with this unexpected and formidable opposition, Hesse agreed to a truce and opened discussions for the withdrawal of his troops.[58]

Gustavus was spared what might have been a military, diplomatic, and constitutional debacle. As the Prussians and British pulled Gustavus from the pit he had dug for himself, he neither asked for nor awaited Louis XVI's opinion. Indeed, for the most part, his ally was completely out of the picture. Pons at Stockholm knew nothing about what was happening. Gustavus later pleaded with Versailles to forgive him for having thrown himself into the arms of Elliot. But, he explained to Pons, he was in such great danger he found it impossible to reject so effective a mediation as that of Prussia united with Britain. Pons, thoroughly mortified by the ineffective role he had played in the critical mediations, begged

---

56. Pons to Montmorin, 7 October 1788, AAE-cp-Suède, 281:267–74vo.

57. Minto, *Memoir*, 307.

58. Ibid., 311; Pons to Montmorin, 21, 28 October 1788, AAE-cp-Suède, 281:299–304vo, 307–10; LaHouze to Montmorin, 28 October 1788, AAE-cp-Dannemark, 166:411.

Versailles for instructions. But he later admitted he was not sure he would be listened to any longer at Stockholm.[59]

The Swedish king returned to Stockholm to face the domestic and constitutional problems he had been trying to avoid.[60] He soon provoked another constitutional crisis and further augmented his powers by granting privileges to the bourgeoisie and peasants at the expense of the nobles. Believing he had frustrated his enemies and consolidated his authority at home, he once again took up his war against Russia. An assassin brought him down in 1792.

Before that tragic murder, as the revolutionary crisis in France deepened in the fall of 1789, Gustavus began secret negotiations with Louis XVI to renew the 1784 Franco-Swedish treaty of alliance. Through his agent, the baron de Taube, Gustavus offered to send a naval squadron to the English Channel to help Louis discipline his rebellious subjects. On his part, Louis XVI had only to break his alliance with Austria and increase his subsidies to Sweden. But by now Louis XVI had little confidence in Gustavus as an ally. He had, furthermore, no money for subsidies. In any case, the domestic crisis in France made it difficult to pursue routine diplomatic matters with anyone. As Madame de Stael wrote to Gustavus: "We suffer here from lack of money, from the dearness of bread; the authority of the king is almost entirely lost ... , the disunion between the different orders of the State is general; a violent crisis approaches."[61]

59. Pons to Montmorin, 7 October, 4 November 1788, AAE-cp-Suède, 281:269–71, 312–18.

60. Minto, *Memoir*, 73–74.

61. Geffroy, *Gustave III et la Cour de France*, 86–87.

PART III

Public Opinion

NINE

Public Opinion and the Desacralization of Diplomacy

"PUBLIC OPINION," the nineteenth-century clergyman William R. Inge once remarked, is "a vulgar, impertinent and anonymous tyrant." And Louis XVI, we might add for contrast, was a well-mannered, gentle, and just monarch. In the later part of the eighteenth century, the two—the tyrant and the monarch—engaged in what proved to be mortal combat. The tyrant won. As the French historian Albert Sorel observed, the French abdicated their political rights to the absolute monarchy, but they never abdicated their powers of judgment.[1]

That public opinion was an important element in the political life of eighteenth-century France is no longer debated. Historians recognize, also, that eighteenth-century public opinion and government control and censorship had a history going back at least to Louis XIII.[2] But historians need to broaden the range of issues that engaged public opinion to include foreign affairs and diplomacy. The literate public—composed of wealthy bourgeoisie and

1. Albert Sorel, *L'Europe et la Révolution Française* (Paris, 1885), 1:195.
2. See, for example: Howard M. Solomon, *Public Welfare, Science and Propaganda in Seventeenth Century France: The Innovation of Theophraste Renaudot* (Princeton, 1972); Joseph Klaits, *Printed Propaganda under Louis XIV, Absolute Monarchy and Public Opinion* (Princeton, 1976).

aristocrats, men of letters, ecclesiastics, judges, military men, diplomats, and government officials who composed the base of public opinion—read about, discussed, and criticized their government's foreign policies, its diplomatic practices, and its ministers and agents.[3] But the size of this elite is difficult to determine. One estimate, based on the number of those people who bought one or more books a year and, perhaps, subscribed to a newspaper, is that the literate public numbered between 30,000 and 50,000 people.[4] Readers of cosmopolitan newspapers, such as the *Gazette de Leyde*, were a smaller, but very influential, percentage of that reading public.[5]

As public opinion grew in importance, French men and women became accustomed to the idea that the monarchy and the men who represented it were subject to the scrutiny of critical reason and the judgments of morality. Over time, discussion, criticism, and debate informed a public that grew increasingly disenchanted with the government and the king's ministers.[6] The monarch, his family, his officials, and their policies eventually became the objects not only of criticism but of satire, ridicule, and obscene libel.[7] The Divine Right Monarchy was no longer sacred.

3. Jeremy D. Popkin, *News and Politics in the Age of Revolution: Jean Luzac's 'Gazette de Leyde'* (Ithaca, N.Y., 1989), 120–32; Charles Gomel, *Les Causes Financières de la Révolution Francaise* (Paris, 1892), 1:ix-x.

4. Raymond Birn, "Livre et Société after Ten Years: Formation of a Discipline," *Studies on Voltaire and the Eighteenth Century* 151 (1976): 294. Other historians of French public opinion, such as Jeremy Popkin, apparently agree that Birn's estimate is about as close to accurate as the evidence permits. See: Jeremy Popkin, "The French Revolutionary Press: New Findings and New Perspectives," *Eighteenth-Century-Life* 5(4) (Summer 1979): 96. While Jack Censer agrees that this estimate "may be reasonable," he concedes that "it is no more than an educated guess." Jack R. Censer and Jeremy D. Popkin, eds., *Press and Politics in Pre-Revolutionary France* (Berkeley, 1987), 22.

5. Popkin, *News and Politics*, 120.

6. William Doyle, *Origins of the French Revolution* (Oxford, 1980), 25–26.

7. Robert Darnton, "Reading, Writing, and Publishing in Eighteenth-Century France," *Daedalus* 100 (1976): 241–56.

Thus, the political culture of the French Revolution developed within the bosom of the Old Regime. In theory judged only by God, the French monarch in the last decades of the eighteenth century faced judgment before the court of public opinion.[8] In the same way, diplomatic affairs and foreign policy, long the exclusive domain of aristocrats, closed *cabinets*, and the most secret and sacred reserve of the king, were reported and discussed in salons, brochures, books, and journals and, consequently, also became the subject for debate and public criticism.

Before the court of public opinion, the image of the monarch and his ministers suffered, even provoked contempt. Both fact and fiction generated pictures of a weak king absorbed in hunting, daily ceremonials, and other trivial pursuits and openly manipulated, especially in foreign affairs, by an ambitious and arrogant queen. Nor was the rot confined to government. A stock market scandal that occurred in the last years of the Old Regime illustrates the point.

Trading in government bonds (as well as joint stock shares) on the Paris stock exchange was frequently carried on in an atmosphere of speculative frenzy. On one occasion, the finance minister Calonne, fearing a collapse of the market, intervened and bought up tumbling stocks in order to support prices and prevent a wholesale collapse of the market. Predictably, his manipulations leaked into the public domain. The result: a disgraceful scandal involving not only important government officials, such as Calonne, but also many clergymen, nobles, and respected banking and commercial houses. As the affair played out it public opinion, it diminished trust in the government and shook public confidence.[9]

8. Keith Michael Baker, "Politics and Public Opinion under the Old Regime: Some Reflections," in Jack R. Censer and Jeremy D. Popkin, eds., *Press and Politics*, 212. Baker treats these issues more fully in his *Inventing the French Revolution* (Cambridge, England, 1992).

9. George V. Taylor, "The Paris Bourse on the Eve of the French Revolution, 1781–1789," *American Historical Review* 67 (1961–62): 951–77. Speculation in French securities was not limited to Paris: see James C. Riley, "Dutch Investments in France, 1781–1787," *Journal of Economic History* 33, no. 4 (December 1973), 732–60.

As public opinion became important in French political culture, the king and his officials responded by trying to influence it. They became participants, although not always effective participants, in the formation of public opinion. They would govern, apparently, by leading public opinion. Royal edicts were printed in newspapers and introduced with long preambles to justify and explain royal polices. Royal ministers and their paid apologists published brochures, pamphlets, and volumes of books defending government policies. Government-sponsored newspapers published information approved and polished by officials.[10]

Opinion about France's foreign affairs and diplomacy on the eve of the Revolution developed within a long tradition of distrust. The French moralist La Bruyère set the tone in the seventeenth century when he noted that the diplomat was an unreliable character. He was a "chameleon" able to assume different personalities to fit the time, place, occasion, as well as the temperament and character of the country and persons with whom he negotiated— all to achieve his ends, which were to deceive others and avoid being deceived himself.[11]

Later, *philosophes* touched the heart of the matter by questioning fundamental assumptions about diplomacy and foreign relations. They deplored the thinking that gave foreign affairs priority over the most pressing domestic issues. And they considered as "dangerous prejudices" the value put on the "military virtues" which enforced diplomatic power.[12] While most diplomats saw war as an instrument, admittedly costly but altogether acceptable as a means to

10. Keith Michael Baker, "Politics and Public Opinion," 212; Robert Darnton, "Reading, Writing, and Publishing," 240. The French government's attempts to control the press and influence public opinion were not new to the eighteenth century: see Solomon and Klaits, cited above.

11. Quoted in Albert Sorel, *L'Europe et la Révolution Française* (Paris, 1885), 1:21–22. Sorel apparently believed that La Bruyère's writings would make a useful manual for diplomacy.

12. Felix Gilbert, "The 'New' Diplomacy of the Eighteenth Century," *World Politics* 5, no. 1 (October 1951), 6.

achieve the ends of the state, critics such as Voltaire, Saint Priest, and Turgot saw war as an extravagantly expensive enterprise, a mistake, a danger, an immorality, even a crime. Pushing the analysis even further, critics demanded that France change its priorities in order to concentrate on domestic reform rather than international power and influence. "Flatterers assure princes," concluded the marquis d'Argenson, "that the interior is there only to serve foreign policy. Duty tells us the opposite. . . . The true purpose of the science called politics is to perfect the interior of a state as much as possible."[13] Mirabeau, the future revolutionary, agreed. There could be no effective foreign policies, he wrote, unless there was a strong domestic base.[14] Even a fundamental concept of Old Regime diplomacy, the balance of power, was attacked. Balance of power did not serve peace, critics said. Instead, it produced perpetual instability and violence.[15]

French diplomacy in the Old Regime was the domain of monarchs, aristocracy, and privilege. Most of the ambassadors who represented the courts of Europe and negotiated the alliances and peace treaties were nobles, who enjoyed special privileges in the hierarchies of their own societies. In addition, as diplomats they enjoyed extensive privileges and immunities in the larger international community and in the host countries where they dwelt. Thus, in their personal as well as official capacities they lived outside many of the civil and criminal laws respected by the rest of mankind.

The identification in the public's eye of aristocrats with diplomacy was not a blessing for the reputation of diplomatic affairs. As

13. Marquis d'Argenson, *Considérations sur le gouvernment ancien et présent de la France* (Amsterdam, 1765), 18; Gilbert, "The 'New' Diplomacy," 7.

14. Quoted in Albert Sorel, *L'Europe et la Révolution Française*, 1:317.

15. See, for example, Gaillard, *Mélanges* (Paris, 1806), 1:7; Charles Edward Vaughan, ed., *The Political Writings of Jean Jacques Rousseau* (Cambridge, Mass., 1915), 1:369; Raynal, *Histoire philosophiques et politiques des etablissements et du commerce des Européannes dans les deux Indes* (Geneva, 1781), 6, 284.

the *philosophes* and public opinion in France developed an elaborate critique of privilege, diplomats and diplomacy were drawn into the crossfire. Such criticism, of course, was not new. Early in the seventeenth century, Sir Henry Wotton provided critics of diplomats with the famous aphorism, "An ambassador is an honest man, sent to lie abroad for the good of his country." What was new in eighteenth-century France was the intensity of the criticism, the circulation it enjoyed among the literate public, and the long-term consequences in French politics.[16]

The *philosophes* were the most articulate spokesmen for the opinion that diplomacy and diplomats did not deserve the public's respect, because they lacked moral purpose. Montesquieu, Holbach, and Diderot all agreed that diplomacy was a sordid activity pursued by morally warped creatures. Rousseau concluded that in diplomacy the Christian courts of Europe recognized "no bonds except their own interests." The politics of diplomacy, Voltaire told his readers, was the "art of lying at the right time."[17] From this position it was not far to the conclusion that aristocratic diplomats did not deserve the privileges they universally enjoyed. Writers and theorists of the Renaissance spoke of the sacred character of the legate or diplomatic envoy. Anyone who injured a diplomat committed a sacrilege.[18] Now, like the monarch of France, the diplomat was "desacralized." He was a liar and a spy, an egoist who enjoyed

16. This cynical view of diplomacy and diplomats endures. In 1954, a French Foreign Office press officer defined his job as "mentir et dementir." And, of course, there is the well-known ditty: "Diplomacy is to do and say / the nastiest things in the nicest way."

17. For the information concerning attitudes of philosophes toward diplomats, I am indebted to Professors Linda and Marsha Frey. They have allowed me to read the preliminary results of their research, which were presented in a paper delivered at the annual meeting of the Society for French Historical Studies, March 29–April 1, 1990, at Columbus, Ohio.

18. Linda Frey and Marsha Frey, "Fatal Diplomacy, 1541," *History Today* 40 (August 1990): 14.

privileges he did not deserve, a charlatan forever occupied with ceremony, ritual, and protocol.

As the decade of the 1780s closed, diplomats and the foreign policy of France suffered from an additional stigma: a series of failures, one of which was the humiliating retreat in the Dutch Republic. Now, more than ever, the diplomat and his activities seemed unworthy of his perquisites and privileges. By 1789, he was a vulnerable target of revolutionaries, who rejected traditional diplomacy altogether and set out to replace it with a new diplomatic system — a system in which, according to Robespierre, ethics were "substituted for egoism, integrity for honor, principles for habits, duties for protocol" and "truth for wit." With the Revolution, "the reign of the charlatan" would, presumably, be over.[19]

But shapers of public opinion were not content with broad and general criticism of diplomats and diplomacy. They wrote, collected, and published, for the edification of what one of them called "enlightened connoisseurs" and "competent judges,"[20] detailed and damaging assessments of key elements of France's foreign policy. We have already described how the bitter condemnation of the Anglo-French (Eden) Commercial Treaty of 1786 led public opinion to believe that the commercial treaty threatened France with economic ruin and *British* domination. The debate over the Versailles Treaty of 1756 which created a Franco-Austrian Alliance was equally charged. In this case, however, the charge was that the Versailles Treaty brought France diplomatic ruin and *Austrian* domination.

The treaty was the work of the former Austrian ambassador to France, Wenzel von Kaunitz, and the result of a treaty of neutral-

19. Quoted from Linda Frey and Marsha Frey, "The Reign of the Charlatan Is Over": The French Revolutionary Attack on Diplomatic Practice," *Journal of Modern History* 65, no. 4 (December 1993), 712–15.

20. The author was the comte de Broglie. Printed in L. P. Ségur, *Politique de tous les cabinets de l'Europe pendant les règnes de Louis XV et de Louis XVI* (Paris, 1793), 1:149.

ity (Westminster, 1756) between Britain and Prussia. It was also the fruit of Kaunitz's previous efforts at Versailles—he was ambassador there until 1753—to promote, with the help of the king's mistress, Madame de Pompadour, a reconciliation between France and Austria. The Treaty of Westminster immediately caused a rupture between Britain and Russia. Russia could not tolerate having its British ally in this new relationship with Prussia, Russia's principle enemy. At Versailles, the treaty also left France annoyed that Frederick II had apparently abandoned France for Britain. Kaunitz skillfully used the indignation to undermine France's confidence in Frederick and to create a rupture between Prussia and France. The result of this complicated diplomatic dance was the Treaty of Versailles, a defensive alliance between France and Austria signed in May of 1756.

But from the moment of its signing, the Franco-Austrian alliance divided the French diplomatic community and its elite observers. In August of the year it was signed, the publicist Jean-Louis Favier attacked it in a memoir requested by the comte d'Argenson, then a minister of Louis XV's government. Favier was an embassy secretary, a secret agent in Louis XV's diplomatic corps, and a man with a dubious reputation.[21] According to the comte de Broglie, he was one of "the most drunken, most debauched and the most deranged of men."[22] But Favier also had a sharp, critical mind and he wrote with a skillful pen. Argenson had warned him when he commissioned the memoir that Louis XV was incapable of sustained attention; Favier therefore organized

21. Jean-Pierre Samoyault, *Les bureaux du secrétariat d'état des affaires étrangères sous Louis XVI* (Paris, 1971), 105–8; Jean-Louis Favier was the author of *Doutes et questions sur le traité de 1756* (Paris, 1756) and at the request of the comte de Broglie he wrote *Conjectures raisonnées sur la situation actuelle de la France dans le système de l'Europe*. The latter work was completed in 1773 and later presented to Louis XVI. It was not published until 1793, but it circulated in Paris in the intervening years. Albert Sorel, *L'Europe et la Révolution Française*, 1:306–8 and 307n.

22. Didier Ozanam and Michel Antoine, *Correspondance secrète du Comte de Broglie avec Louis XV (1756–1774)* (Paris, 1961), 2:431.

the requested memoir into a sequence of simple questions about the treaty followed by short, pithy answers—just the kind of writing the reading public enjoyed.[23]

The treaty, Favier claimed, was neither necessary nor beneficial to France's security. In fact, it was dangerous. The two powers had agreed to support each other in case one of them was attacked. But Austria could be attacked by the armies of Prussia, Russia, the German Empire, Holland, Turkey, the king of Naples or the king of Sardinia. The only land power in a position to attack France, Favier pointed out, was Austria itself.[24] Louis XV's official historian, Charles Pinot Duclos, added additional criticism. The Austrian alliance and the Seven Years' War that followed, he claimed, was the work of intriguing Austrians, irresponsible French ministers, and Louis XV's mistress; it was, in short, the "most unfortunate and humiliating event of . . . [Louis XV's] reign." Austria wanted the treaty, he continued, only to bring France into her quarrel with Prussia and to trap France into sharing the expenses of the war. Furthermore, the treaty engaged France to spend its resources in a continental war, thereby making it impossible to wage an effective naval war against Britain.[25] As his critique developed, Duclos made no attempt to restrain his contempt. Who were the "instruments" employed to carry out the despised treaty? "Armchair generals greedy for money, inexperienced or presumptuous men, ignorant, jealous or malicious ministers, subalterns extravagant with their own blood on the battle field but who, at court, crawled before those who gave them favors.[26] French foreign pol-

---

23. L. P. Ségur, *Politique de tous les cabinets de l'Europe*, 3:254.

24. Jean-Louis Favier, *Doutes et questions sur le traité de Versailles du 1er mai, 1756.* Printed in *Politique de tous les cabinets de l'Europe*, 3:251–366. Favier's critic, L. P. Ségur, found Favier's conclusions "un peu outré," his fears exaggerated, and his predictions unjustified (*Politique de tous les cabinets de l'Europe*, 3:300).

25. Charles Pinot Duclos, *Mémoires secret sur les règnes de Louis XIV et de Louis XV* (Paris, 1791), 397, 414. Duclos's *Mémoires* circulated among readers long before it was printed.

26. Ibid., 428.

icy, Favier and Duclos obviously believed, was not in the hands of capable men.

Because of France's persistent resistance to Austrian expansion, the treaty of 1756 was nearly lifeless by the 1780s. But while the alliance had become a shadowy reality in the courts of Europe, it continued to be the subject of an acrimonious and public debate in France. Opponents were not satisfied that, in fact, the alliance had all but unraveled. They wanted France to publicly denounce and officially deny the pact and to seek an alliance with Prussia. The alliance with Austria, the French diplomat the comte de Broglie lamented, had started a "steady deterioration of France's credit, consideration and influence in Europe."[27]

Critics of French foreign policy repeated again and again that the major cause of France's diplomatic failures was the stubborn refusal of Louis XV and Louis XVI to abandon the "Austrian System" and build another diplomatic "federation" with Prussia. After the treaty of 1756, Favier argued, it was impossible to hide the rapid degradation of France in the courts of Europe.[28] As a result of the treaty, France had become a secondary power in the political order. "In short, a reserve corps under Austrian orders."[29] (As Favier warmed to his critique of the treaty, he honed his vocabulary to a sharp edge. "A popular writer," one of his critics noted, he wrote with "his passions . . . , rather than the light of reason.")[30] Austria had achieved a primary place in Europe's politics on the "ruins" of France's former place. All of Europe watched, Favier said, as France sank into a "servile dependence" on Austria.

27. Comte de Broglie, "Mémoire adressé par le Comte de Broglie à MM. les Comte de Muy et de Vergennes, 1 Mars, 1775," printed in *Politique de tous les cabinets de l'Europe*, 1:145.

28. Jean-Louis Favier, "Conjectures raisonnées sur la situation actuelle de la France dans le système politique de l'Europe," printed in *Politique de tous les cabinets de l'Europe*, 1:178.

29. Ibid., 1:182.

30. The critic was L. P. Ségur in his 1801 edition of *Politique de tous les cabinets de l'Europe*, 3:311.

After Louis XV's death and Madame de Pompadour's disappearance from court, Louis XVI continued to recognize the treaty. Who, now, made up the "chain of intrigues" binding France to this continuing public "humiliation?"[31] The answer: "The Austrian," Marie Antoinette. The treaty, critics explained, was much more valuable to Marie Antoinette's relatives—especially her brother Joseph II—in Vienna than to her offspring in France, one of whom would someday inherit the French throne. In 1785, the Paris bookseller Ruault wrote to his brother, "She [Marie Antoinette] has intrigued most energetically on her brother's behalf, against the interests of the House [Bourbon] of which she is sovereign."[32] Marie Antoinette was nothing more than an agent of Austria.[33] The queen's advocacy of the Franco-Austrian alliance was seen not as a personal indiscretion or a case of exaggerated family loyalty, but as treason.[34]

There is no doubt that Marie Antoinette's mother, Maria Theresa, and her brother, Joseph II, expected her to be their spokesperson at Versailles. And, furthermore, there is no doubt that the queen tried to exert the influence and achieve the aims laid out in Vienna's instructions to her and to Mercy, the Austrian ambassador at Versailles. But her attempts to influence Louis XVI's foreign policy, her confrontations with Louis XVI and his ministers to get them to support Vienna, and her repeated attempts to blunt French determination to frustrate Austrian expansion in Poland, or Bavaria or Turkey, ended, for the most part, in failure.[35] Nevertheless, her friends as well as her enemies continued to be-

31. Ibid., 1:187, 188, 374, 417.

32. Claude Manceron, *The French Revoluton: Toward the Brink, 1785–1787* (New York, 1983), 105.

33. Albert Sorel, *L'Europe et la Révolution Française*, 1:305.

34. Ibid., 1:304.

35. The gap between what Maria Theresa and Joseph II expected of Marie Antoinette and what she was able to achieve is described in detail in Jeanne Arnaud-Bouteloup, *Le rôle politique de Marie Anoinette* (Paris, 1929). See especially: 45–60, 73–92, 93–116, 117–45, 161–82.

lieve that Louis XVI's foreign policies originated in Vienna and were implemented at Versailles by a domineering queen. She became the object of universal hatred. Even those who associated with her were hated. Even the rabbits who ran in front of her horses were hated, according to Madame de Chastenay.[36]

Critics such as Favier and Duclos planted the seeds of the charges of treason which French Revolutionaries later brought against Marie Antoinette.[37] During the secret questioning before her trial, her interrogator repeated the public's conviction that she was disloyal to France: "You had, before the revolution, relations with the king of Bohemia and Hungary [i.e. Joseph II] and these relations were contrary to the interests of France. . . ?" Marie answered that the king of Bohemia and Hungary was her brother and her relations with him were out of friendship and not political. But the suspicion of treason would not go away. When the indictment was prepared the charge reappeared: "Marie Antoinette, widow of Louis Capet, has been since her arrival in France the scourge and pain of Frenchmen. Even before the fortunate revolution . . . she had political contacts with the man called the king of Bohemia and Hungary."[38] Thus, revolutionary critics of French foreign policy transformed foreign policy debates, diplomatic events, and even treaty articles into briefs for the prosecution.

The monarchy of France had the legal authority to shape public opinion regarding its diplomatic practices and it could exercise that authority by controlling the distribution of information. It censored publications and asserted its right to prevent the publication and sale of materials unauthorized by the censor. Officialdom influenced the flow of information with its own privileged publications, such as the *Gazette de France*, which published only the information

36. Madame de Chastenay, *Mémoires* (Paris, 1894), 1:89.

37. Sorel, *L'Europe et la Révolution Française*, 1:304. A few French historians continue to insist that the queen was guilty of treason. See, for example, Claude Manceron, *The French Revolution: Toward the Brink, 1785–1787*, 101.

38. Henri Coston, *Procès de Louis XVI et de Marie Antoinette* (Paris, 1981), 644, 657.

the government wanted the public to know. But the government's right to control was difficult to implement and not always effective. Furthermore, the government undermined its own monopoly by allowing newspapers from outside France to circulate freely in France. By the mid-eighteenth century, the literate public read a range of newspapers that monitored actions of the government and publicized reports about foreign affairs and diplomacy, often with critical comment.[39] And even the government-controlled *Gazette de France* printed material that (to the alert and thoughtful reader) undermined confidence in Louis XVI's handling of foreign affairs. The reporting in the *Gazette de France* of the failure of French diplomacy in the Dutch Republic in 1787 illustrates the point.[40]

By the summer of 1787, the long-smoldering disagreements between the Stadholder William V and the Dutch States General approached flash point. In July, the *Gazette de France* reported, the Assembly of the States of Holland had before it a resolution requesting Louis XVI's mediation to help settle the disagreements. Twelve cities in the province of Holland supported the resolution, including the larger cities of Amsterdam, Rotterdam, and Haarlem. If the resolution received approval, it would be carried to the States General of the Dutch Republic. The report further stated that the province of Holland was busily forming new regiments of its army to defend its interests against the stadholder. Thus, the report reminded readers of Louis XVI's position as ally of the Dutch Republic and his role as arbiter in European affairs.[41]

39. Jack R. Censer and Jeremy D. Popkin, "Historians and the Press," in Jack R. Censer and Jeremy D. Popkin, eds., *Press and Politics*, 21.

40. Just as the diplomatic crisis in the Dutch Republic heated up, Charles-Joseph Panckoucke became the director of the *Gazette de France*. Panckoucke, descended from a dynasty of printers and publishers, held the directorship of the *Gazette* until 1792. This acquisition, a part of a veritable publishing empire, was only one of his many publishing and printing ventures. Jean Sgard, *Dictionnaire des Journalistes: 1600–1789* (Grenoble, 1979), 295–97.

41. *Gazette de France*, 10 July, 17 July 1787, 271–72, 283. Hereafter referred to as *GdeF*.

Reports dated July also described an incident that was to be the justification for war. The princess stadholder (also the sister of Frederick William II of Prussia), on her way to the Hague was detained by a detachment of pro-Patriot, auxiliary troops under the orders of the States of Holland. The Patriots refused to allow her to continue to the Hague, but they offered to conduct her to Woerdan, where, they assured her, she could count on all the honor and respect due her "sex, rank, and birth." The princess, however, saw the detainment and the Patriots' offer as an affront to her personal dignity and rank. According to the *Gazette de France*, when she explained her indignation to the public, her rather ominous explanation was that she was trying to prevent a civil war. The very next day the stadholder, determined to punish the actions of the Patriots, occupied the Dutch city of Wyck. This "extraordinary event," commented the reporter of *The Gazette de France*, caused a sensation at the very moment when the province of Holland was trying to arrange a general pacification initiated by the mediation of France, "a friendly and allied power."[42]

Readers of the *Gazette de France* were by now aware that the situation in the Dutch Republic had the potential for civil war and that France, "a friendly and allied power," had intervened to mediate. Just days later, the news from the Dutch Republic raised once again the specter of a civil war with descriptions of how the Orangists supporting the stadholder had begun pillaging homes of the Patriots. In retaliation, soldiers of the States of Holland acted to repress these "excesses." Meanwhile, the king of Prussia's minister publicly demanded satisfaction for the detainment and insult to Frederick William II's sister.[43] While we know from other evidence that this news created a sensation in the ministerial *bureaux* at Versailles, there was nothing in the *Gazette de France* to indicate how—or even *if*—Louis XVI had responded to the developments

42. Ibid., 13 July, 17 July 1787, 279, 283.
43. Ibid., 20 July 1787, 287.

in the Dutch Republic. Instead, in the pages of this official journal, we read of Louis XVI absorbed in the routine ceremonies and rituals of Versailles. He busily nominated clergymen to various dioceses. The queen visited the Trianon with Elizabeth de France.[44] Shortly afterwards, Harris, the British ambassador to the Dutch Republic, presented a memoir to the Dutch States General informing them that His Britannic Majesty was pleased that the Dutch were thinking of ending the fighting by mediation. Several provinces, Harris noted, had indicated they wanted British mediation, and Harris let them know that he was prepared to provide it.[45] Harris's suggestion that the king of Great Britain mediate a settlement of the Dutch question was an undisguised challenge to Louis XVI.

Less than a month after the report of Harris's statement, the *Gazette de France* announced that the maréchal de Ségur had resigned as secretary of state for the army and the maréchal de Castries had also resigned as secretary of state for the navy. The comte de Saint Priest had been appointed as ambassador to the Dutch Republic, to fill the position just recently vacated by the marquis de Vérac. These news items were the only evidence in the *Gazette de France*'s reports from Versailles that a diplomatic crisis of major proportions had left the king's diplomacy in disarray and divided his ministry. Yet, apparently, the daily life of His Majesty had not been disturbed. The king, the *Gazette de France* reported, preoccupied with family responsibilities, had just signed the marriage contract of the comte de Polignac and the demoiselle de Livry.[46]

In September of 1787 the Prussian King Frederick William II, still claiming that the incident involving his sister was an affront to family honor, ordered his troops to invade the Dutch Republic. And there was disturbing news from London. The English Admiralty had ordered the navy put on a war footing. The War Office

44. Ibid.   45. Ibid., 10 August 1787, 345.
46. Ibid., 7 September 1787, 359.

told the Guards and infantry to assemble all troops for inspection. Orders were issued for the impressment of sailors for the fleet and returning merchant ships found themselves emptied of able-bodied sailors, who were impressed onto naval ships. Extra dock workers had been hired to equip and supply some of England's largest ships of the line. On 16 October 1787, the news from London informed readers of the *Gazette de France* that all the garrisons of the north and west of England were being increased and "put on a war footing." By the first week in October, the impressment of sailors for the fleet was extended to Ireland. By late October 1787, the *Gazette de France* reported that everything in the port of Plymouth, England, "seemed to announce war." In November, all officers of the fleet had been ordered to report to their departments to receive orders.[47] Meanwhile, during the first week of October, the *Gazette de France* had announced that most of the opposition to the Prussians and the stadholder had disappeared. Only the city of Amsterdam continued to hold out.[48] A month later, resistance had vanished. The pro-French Patriots were no longer a political force in the Dutch Republic. Prussian troops occupied the province of Holland and the Prussian general, the duke of Brunswick, made preparations to winter there.[49] Thus, *The Gazette de France* presented to its readers the public humiliation of Louis XVI and his allies in the Dutch Republic.

While readers of the *Gazette de France* learned in the items from London that George III energetically prepared for war to back his friends in the Dutch Republic, they found (sometimes on the same pages) Louis XVI playing an altogether different role. The *Gazette de France* described his participation in court ceremonials, his con-

47. The news items describing England's preparations for war are in the *GdeF*, 14, 20 September; 5, 9, 12, 19, 26 October; 2, 6, 9, 16 November 1787. Indications, even the most indirect indications, of Louis XVI's responses to the threatening war are sparse. See: 16 January; 16 and "Supplément," 19 October; 16 November 1787.

48. Ibid., 5 October 1787, 395.   49. Ibid., 9 November 1787, 445.

cern for family affairs, his official ordinances, decrees, and edicts concerning finances, taxes, the establishment of provincial assemblies and commerce in grain. The newspaper printed in full the discourses of the king and leading notables at the Assembly of Notables. But readers had to scan the pages carefully for any evidence of Louis XVI's role in the diplomatic crisis in the Dutch Republic. What coverage there was, was sparse, indifferent, and undeveloped. The king of France as arbiter of Europe was scarcely visible.

Finally, in mid-November, the *Gazette de France* reported the sorry end of the tale. "[A]s a consequence of declarations and counter-declarations" signed by representatives of the kings of Britain and France and exchanged at Versailles, French naval preparations for war had been discontinued.[50] Thus, readers of the *Gazette de France* learned for the first time that France, too, had prepared for war. From then until the end of the year 1787, the *Gazette de France* provided readers very little information about the fate of French interests in the Dutch Republic.

We know from other evidence that Louis XVI was very much involved in the agonizingly difficult decisions concerning the Dutch crisis. But the government newspaper did not share with the public this important part of the monarch's responsibilities. His day-to-day activities, as reported by the official journal, were concerned with other matters. In fact, readers of the *Gazette de France* learned in much greater detail how the British government responded to the Dutch crisis.

An age-old tradition in France placed foreign policy and diplomacy among the king's exclusive prerogatives. They were secret and, therefore, not open to public view. Foreign affairs, the historian Albert Sorel correctly noted, belonged to the king's "royal world, to his caste, to his family; in short [foreign affairs] belonged to his own private affairs."[51] But in observing the tradition, the

50. Ibid., 16 November 1787, 453.
51. Albert Sorel, *L'Europe et la Révolution Française*, 1:299.

Gazette de France may very well have communicated to its readers an image of the king which it did not intend: that of a man indifferent to foreign affairs and doing nothing to defend France's interests and prestige abroad. Having decided to rule with the support of public opinion, Louis XVI failed to provide the public with the slightest glimpse of one of his most important concerns and activities: his goals, motivations, and actions in foreign affairs.

Readers of the *Gazette de France* therefore found in the newspaper perceptions of Louis XVI that were in sharp contrast to his own image of himself as arbiter of Europe. "The purpose of this kind of journalism," the historian Jeremy Popkin concludes, "was not to make the king's actions rationally comprehensible but simply to render them visible."[52] In this case, official journalism made visible a king who apparently did not participate in the decisions affecting France's role in international affairs. Inevitably, that meant that the public would get its news about France's foreign affairs from other sources, including such newspapers as the Dutch *Gazette de Leyde*, which saw foreign affairs as a very serious matter, indeed.

52. Jeremy Popkin's *News and Politics in the Age of Revolution*, 47–48.

TEN

Public Opinion: The King Is a "Nullity"

NEWS IN the *Gazette de France* provided the reader with a selected and very limited pool of information from which to interpret diplomatic events. Readers of the Dutch newspaper, *Gazette de Leyde*, however, found in its columns full accounts of French diplomatic affairs provided by the French correspondent, Pascal Boyer, by military and diplomatic professionals, officials within the royal ministries and private parties.[1] Published in the Dutch city of Leiden, it was better informed about what happened in France than any other newspaper, and it distributed its news largely free of the French government's restrictions. The *Gazette De Leyde* was one of the most influential of the foreign newspapers in France. It was read by wealthy French bourgeoisie and aristocrats, members of the royal family, the court, even by the king himself.[2] The *Gazette de Leyde* was, according to Jeremy Popkin, a major force in the development of French public opinion.[3]

French foreign affairs and diplomacy was one of the topics most

1. Jeremy D. Popkin, *News and Politics in the Age of Revolution: Jean Luzac's 'Gazette de Leyde'* (Ithaca, N.Y., 1989), 47, 71–75, 129.

2. Ibid., 7, 126–29.

3. Jeremy D. Popkin, "The *Gazette de Leyde* and French Politics under Louis XVI," in Jack R. Censer and Jeremy D. Popkin, eds., *Press and Politics in Pre-Revolutionary France* (Berkeley, 1987), 88–89.

frequently treated in the *Gazette de Leyde*. While the *Gazette de Leyde* generally cultivated a calm and objective tone in reporting the international news, the Dutch crisis, which came to a head in 1787, was too close to home to permit objectivity.[4] News coming out of Dutch cities was biased in favor of the Patriots, and news from Paris and Versailles dwelt at length on the responses of the French government, which was committed by treaty to support the Patriots. The reports and comments of the London correspondent in the same newspaper, however, usually contained an altogether different perspective. Thus, in late 1786 and early 1787, when the British and the French were in sharp competition to see who would complete a commercial treaty with Russia, the London correspondent who thought—prematurely it turned out—a British-Russian commercial treaty was near completion, boasted that "all the credit and effort of the Court of France at [St.] Petersburg would never procure for French commerce in Russia the particular and exclusive advantages which gave the English a grand superiority in that country."[5] A few weeks later, however, the Paris correspondent announced in his column that "everyone" at the French court was praising and complimenting the French secretaries of state for their success in completing a commercial treaty with Russia.[6]

Throughout the reporting of the crisis year 1787 the London and French correspondents of the *Gazette de Leyde* presented their own capital's version of events and even slanted their reports in such a way to suggest that they were, in fact, responding to each

4. The editor of the *Gazette de Leyde*, Jean Luzac, and members of his family were divided in their opinions of the stadholder and the Patriot party. Luzac generally supported the moderate Patriots until the intervention of the Prussian army. He responded to the Prussian invasion by supporting more radical solutions to the political conflict: see Popkin, *News and Politics*, 15–23, 167–87.

5. *Gazette de Leyde ou Nouvelles Extraordinaire de divers endroits*. London, 22 December 1786 (edition of 2 January 1787). Hereafter referred to as *GdeL*.

6. Ibid., Paris, 5 February 1787 (edition of 13 February 1787).

other. Sometimes the reader cannot avoid the impression that individuals within the ministries of the two countries were actually carrying on a public slanging match with each other in the pages of the newspaper.

The competition between Britain and France was reflected in the *Gazette de Leyde* in still another way. Both monarchs were involved in reforming their finances, each was rebuilding its navy to influence diplomatic affairs, and each was deeply involved in the political and constitutional conflict in the Dutch Republic. Thus readers of the *Gazette de Leyde* were spectators, so to speak, at an international contest to see whether France or England could best cope with these dramatic issues.

Just before the opening of the British Parliament in December 1786, the London correspondent reported that there was great impatience in London concerning Pitt's proposals for financial reforms. There would be a huge deficit, the correspondent believed, and there would undoubtedly be a "new plan of taxation."[7] Some weeks later, the London correspondent reported that Pitt was still developing his plans to consolidate the public revenues and simplify tax collections. The project, according to the source, had made a striking impression, not only on members of the House of Commons, but also in the nation.[8]

In January of 1787 the Paris correspondent had reported in the *Gazette de Leyde* that Louis XVI had resolved to call an Assembly of Notables, which would concern itself with the "good of the state and the relief of his people." France, too, would deal with its financial problems.[9] As the public waited for the Assembly of Notables to open after several delays, there were rumors, according to the Paris correspondent, of "vast and sublime" projects to abolish fifty million livres of taxes and to redistribute the public tax burden so it

7. Ibid., London, 26 December 1786 (edition of 2 January 1787).
8. Ibid., London, 2 March 1787 (edition of 13 March 1787).
9. Ibid., Versailles, 30 December 1786 (edition of 9 January 1787).

would be more equitable. As the reports and rumors continued to bubble,[10] the Paris correspondent informed his readers that the information now before the public regarding the Assembly of Notables announced "a new order of things," a new order likely to arouse public spirit and create great hopes.[11] Later, the news from Paris said that the great issues treated in the Assembly of Notables and its committees were the only subjects of conversation in Paris, in public places or in private society. These deliberations so preoccupied Paris that "one played little attention to anything else."[12]

By the first week of March, however, the picture was less optimistic. The *Gazette de Leyde* noted that Calonne's plans for reform faced certain opposition; in the same week we learn that the bureaux of the Assembly of Notables had rejected Calonne's plan for a territorial tax.[13] Meanwhile, the *Gazette de Leyde* reported, Monsieur de St. James, a treasurer general of the French navy, had suspended payments from his treasury.[14] The author of the report stressed the fact that when the *Chambre des Comptes* announced the difficulties with the accounts of Monsieur de St. James, it used words such as "derangements" and "momentary embarrassment." The correspondent could not resist pointing out how they carefully avoided using the words "bankruptcy" or "failure."[15]

In the edition of 20 March 1787, readers of the *Gazette de Leyde* read Calonne's controversial conclusion that the finances of the French government had been in disorder when Louis XVI mounted the throne and they were still so in 1786. Despite the value of Necker's reforms, according to the news items on Calonne, the reforms never compensated for the interest on the loans to fight the

10. Ibid., Paris, 2 February 1787 (edition of 9 February 1787).
11. Ibid., Paris, 9 February 1787 (edition of 16 February 1787).
12. Ibid., Paris, 9 March, 1787 (edition of 16 March 1787).
13. Ibid., Versailles, 7,8 March 1787 (edition of 16 March 1787).
14. Ibid., Paris, 5 February 1787 (edition of 13 February 1787).
15. Ibid., Paris, suppl. 12 February 1787 (edition of 20 February 1787).

American War. Thus, the deficit continued to grow.[16] Equally serious, however, was the news that the French *Chambre de Comptes* had examined the accounts of financiers who had suffered financial failure and found "truly alarming" several different bankruptcies which had cost the king about 40 million livres. Moreover, instead of being punished, most of the bankrupt financiers had been compensated, some by being granted pensions, others by appointments to "honorable places." The son of the bankrupt financier Harvoin had actually obtained a pension of 12,000 livres.[17]

By the end of March the London correspondent emphasized the significance of what was happening in France and Britain: it was worthy of remark, he wrote, that France and Britain, for so long rivals in military glory, in power, and in commerce, exhausted finally by long wars that this rivalry had caused, were today joined together in a new friendship trying to reform their finances and correct the vicious aspects of their interior administration.[18] Thus the efforts of Pitt and Calonne were portrayed as historic moments in the history of both countries. When the Assembly of Notables rejected Calonne's plans for reform, news of the failure was immediately published along with the news that Pitt's reforms were "rapidly advancing."[19] The belief that Pitt's reforms were successful was so widespread that the French ambassador in London reported that Pitt had succeeded in balancing the budget.[20] In contrast, readers of the *Gazette de Leyde* soon learned that Calonne

16. Ibid., Paris, 9 March 1787 (edition of 16 March 1787).

17. Ibid., "extrait" from the *Gazette de France*, 18 February 1787 (edition of 27 February 1787).

18. Ibid., London, 30 March 1787 (edition of 10 April 1787).

19. Ibid., London 16, 20, and 23 March 1787 (edition of 23 March 1787). Marie Donaghay, "The Best Laid Plans: French Execution of the Anglo-French Commercial Treaty of 1786," *European History Quarterly* 14 (1984), 406.

20. Ibid., 406; Pitt's biographer, John Ehrman, doubts that Pitt had balanced the budget. He suggests there probably was still a hefty deficit. See: *The Younger Pitt: The Years of Acclaim* (London, 1969), 275–77.

had not only failed but had fled France to England.[21] If a sound financial system was the foundation of influence in international affairs, readers of the *Gazette de Leyde* might very well have concluded that France was sailing into a storm.

As the political conflict between the Patriot party and the stadholder began to boil over in the United Provinces, the Dutch response was to turn to France; they expected Louis XVI to play the role of mediator. A report originating from Leiden insisted that if the stadholder would sacrifice something to the cause of peace and the well-being of his country, there was no one more suited for bringing the parties together than the French minister to The Hague, the marquis de Vérac. But unfortunately, the wishes of this minister, even the wishes of the Prussian envoy, M. de Goertz, appeared to have been frustrated by the inflexibility of the stadholder. Almost two weeks later, the situation had not changed. There was little chance for conciliation as long as the prince of Orange continued to insist that he have all the prerogatives which the stadholder enjoyed before 1780, even if they had been gained by his abuse of power.[22] A few days later another report from Leiden announced that a French representative, M. de Rayneval, had just left The Hague to return to Versailles. He had been sent to Holland to find ways to end the troubles there. Rayneval had tried to convince the king of Prussia that France did not want to take away from the stadholder any of his responsibilities or functions. But this new French attempt to mediate was a pathetic failure. According to the Dutch report, the prince of Orange remained inflexible and all hope of an accommodation mediated by the French had vanished. "[T]he future," said a letter from Paris, "is enveloped in a profound obscurity."[23]

21. *GdeL*, Paris 16 July 1787 (edition of 20 July 1787).

22. Ibid., Leiden, 3 January 1787; The Hague, 14 January 1787 (editions of 2, 16 January 1787).

23. Ibid., Leiden, 17 January 1787; The Hague, 17 January 1787; Paris, 26 January 1787 (editions of 19, 30 January 1787).

After the departure of Rayneval, reports from Paris hinted at divisions within the French government over policy. On the one hand, according to the Paris correspondent, Louis XVI used strong language to warn the prince of Orange that he was creating divisions in his country which France could not tolerate, because of her treaty engagements with the United Provinces.[24] On the other hand, after the death of Vergennes, Louis XVI's secretary of state for foreign affairs, the correspondent from Paris assured the readers of the *Gazette de Leyde* that the political system established by Vergennes, that of "pacification and conciliation," would not change. It was not clear what this meant in the light of other reports from Leiden that the prince of Orange still refused to compromise and would not accept any changes in his prerogatives.[25] Shortly after the 20th of June, when the princess of Orange was detained by the detachments of armed men, the stadholder entered Holland with 3,000 troops.[26] The letter from Versailles contained the French official response: the French Court put a great price on its alliance with the United Provinces and, having acquired the advantages of the alliance, France was resolved to protect it.[27]

The *Gazette de Leyde*'s reports from France that followed were quite possibly written or provided by one or several of the hawks in Louis XVI's cabinet: they are battle cries rather than news. The French ministry, one report stated, had learned that London, ready to defend the stadholder, had armed a naval squadron to back up its intent. So the French ministry had sent orders to Brest to prepare immediately twelve ships of the line and four frigates to match the English squadron. The cabinet of St. James then backed down and France countermanded its orders to Brest. Perhaps England and those in Holland who are attached to England believed,

24. Ibid., Paris, 30 January 1787 (edition of 9 February 1787).

25. Ibid., Leiden, 4 March; The Hague, 3 January 1787 (editions of 6, 16 March, 1787).

26. Ibid., Leiden, 1 July 1787 (edition of 6 July 1787).

27. Ibid., Versailles, 24 June 1787 (edition of 3 July 1787).

wrote the Versailles correspondent, that the state of French finances as reported in the Assembly of Notables gave them a free
hand to mix in the domestic quarrels of a neighbor without title or
reason. "But we have proved to them and we will prove on every
occasion, that a Nation, such as France never lacks the energy and
will never lack the resources, when it is a question of sustaining its
political interests and the honor of its King." The reporter then
added that, while England paraded the annual additions to its
navy, "we are not lagging behind." This manly challenge ended
with the warning, "We have shown [Holland] that we are loyal
allies, and that we will not suffer that any neighbor intervene in
this quarrel against Holland's will ."[28]

Similar reports coming out of Versailles continued to be printed
(as news) in the *Gazette de Leyde* throughout the summer of 1787.
One article solemnly announced: "We do not abandon our friends
in a crisis." When the Versailles correspondent reported that Britain
was harassing French ships in India, French policy seemed to do
an about-face. While an earlier French correspondent assured
readers that Vergennes's policy of conciliation was current policy,
suddenly things were different. With a prudence that sometimes
carried him to the point of timidity, the French reporter declared,
Vergennes would have remained silent in the present crisis. But,
the correspondant assured readers,"our ministers today are less enduring." They will demand satisfaction for each and every trespass
committed by Britain.[29]

When the French government learned of the march of Prussian
troops toward the Dutch border, statements from Versailles became shrill and bellicose. The encampment of French troops at
Givet, the Versailles correspondent warned, was going to be reinforced by eighteen batallions and twenty-three squadrons. Indeed,
these troops were already marching. "Our court believes its honor

28. Ibid., Versailles, 24 June 1787 (edition of 6 July 1787).
29. Ibid., Versailles, 5 July 1787 (edition of 6 July 1787).

is involved."[30] After Prussian troops crossed over onto Dutch soil, a report from The Hague claimed that France had told the Dutch that if the Prussian troops continued their invasion of Holland, His Majesty Louis XVI "was determined, in his quality of ally, to come to the aid of this province."[31] The Paris correspondent reported French troop buildups, naval rearmament, and diplomatic couriers rushing here and there.[32] But when the comte de St. Priest, on his way to The Hague to be France's new ambassador, heard that Prussian troops had crossed the Dutch border, he stopped at Anvers, settled his entourage into comfortable quarters, and sent back to Versailles for new instructions.[33] Despite France's announced determination to aid its allies, more than two weeks after the Prussian invasion the *Gazette de Leyde* reported that Versailles still had not acted. Louis XVI was waiting for his new minister of the army, Brienne, to arrive from Bordeaux.[34]

By now the reports in the *Gazette de Leyde* were hinting that France's response to the Dutch crisis would fall far short of what earlier announcements led readers to expect. A report from Versailles informed readers that the duke of Brunswick and Prussian troops had penetrated deep into Dutch territory. France's new ambassador to the Dutch Republic, however, still had not found his way to The Hague. The new minister, Brienne, had finally arrived from Bordeaux, but he became immediately "indisposed" upon his arrival. Meanwhile, the States General of the Dutch Republic sent a courier to Versailles to announce that, since the return of the stadholder, all past decisions of the States of Holland were null and void. The States General ceremoniously thanked Louis XVI for

---

30. Ibid., London, 14 August; Versailles, 19 August 1787 (editions of 17, 28 August 1787).

31. Ibid., The Hague, 18 September 1787 (edition of 18 September 1787).

32. Ibid., Paris, 17 September 1787 (edition of 25 September 1787).

33. Ibid., Anvers, 22 September 1787 (edition of 28 September 1787).

34. GdeL, Versailles, 23 September 1787 (edition of 28 September 1787).

his offer to mediate, but informed him that the previously requested help was no longer needed.[35]

For the next two weeks, reports from Paris continued to announce, simultaneously, the likelihood of war and the prospects for
peace. Army and naval officers hastily departed from and returned
to Versailles. A French report stated that Britain was determined
to destroy France's alliance with the Dutch Republic and over-
throw the diplomatic edifice that the comte de Vergennes had
spent six years building. A short item noted that both the French
court and Pitt wanted peace and that the aid that France wanted to
give Holland was already too late, "consequently, useless." One correspondent from Paris revealed that all the French armies previously described with great fanfare as forming or marching to
defend the Dutch Republic existed only on paper. Yet, political
tension remained strained. "Something," said one report, "had to
bend or break." Among the news items circulated by the Dutch
newspaper was one which promised that if there was a rupture
with Britain, France was ready to assemble fifty-three ships of the
line at Brest and launch an invasion of England. While the public
discussed such grandiose projects, Louis XVI's council, according to *The Gazette de Leyde*, shrouded its urgent discussions in
secrecy.[36]

Later, even after reports indicated that Britian had begun to
disarm, the Paris correspondent reported that Louis XVI remained
insistent that the Prussian invasion of Dutch territory injured his
dignity as an ally of the United Provinces. War, consequently, appeared inevitable. From Paris came estimates and comparisons of
what the consequences of war might be. Britain would annul the
commercial treaty with France. Her commerce would stagnate.
English taxes would increase. War would mean to France a "very
great misfortune." Never before had the state of French finances

35. Ibid., Versailles, 23 September 1787; Paris, 28 September 1787 (editions of 2,
5 October 1787).

36. Ibid., Paris, 4, 11 October 1787 (editions of 12, 16 October 1787).

required peace as much as they did then. But it appeared that "the honor of the king and national considerations" had been compromised.[37] As for paying for a war with Britain: "[T]he Nation will no doubt shoulder the necessary expenses since the issue is one that it holds the most dear: its own honor and that of the king." France was united in this one sentiment. In fact, zealous military officers at court were so carried away by concern for their king's honor that they were loudly affirming they would go to war and pay for the military campaign out of their own pockets. So generous a devotion, opined the Paris correspondent of the *Gazette de Leyde*, was only too characteristic of the French nobility.[38]

By November 1787, the stadholder was firmly in power, with the Prussian army and, potentially, the British navy solidly behind him. Louis XVI's power to mediate a settlement had evaporated in the heat of events. St. Priest, when he finally reached The Hague, could only hope that "Dutch interests were not entirely sacrificed." But there was still a need to explain, and the *Gazette de Leyde* provided the explanation: France did not intervene because of the state of French finances, because its Austrian allies refused to make a diversion against Prussia and the French Parlement refused to help Louis XVI provide the necessary means for war.[39] The London correspondent of the *Gazette de Leyde* also felt moved to observe, somewhat smugly, that recent events proved that France seemed "prepared to sacrifice a point of honor rather than expose itself to the necessity of a war."[40]

Thus the war of words that took place in the columns of the *Gazette de Leyde* ended with France defeated and Louis XVI's honor sacrificed. The detailed descriptions of French war preparations (some of which existed only on paper), the warlike threats

37. Ibid., Paris, 4, 8, 11, 12 October 1787 (editions of 12, 16, 19 October 1787).

38. Ibid., Paris, 12 October 1787 (edition of 19 October 1787).

39. Ibid., Paris, 25 October, Versailles, 27, 29 October 1787 (editions of 2, 6 November 1787).

40. Ibid., London, 26 October 1787 (edition of 2 November 1787).

and bragging assertions, could only have reinforced the opinion that France was fully prepared to launch another war to protect its honor and its Dutch allies. In reality, however, the real war turned out to be a war of words in the pages of the *Gazette de Leyde*. Nevertheless, the exchanges surely raised expectations about what France was going to do in the crisis. And the expectations were certainly disappointed when Louis XVI did not go to war to defend the Dutch Patriots. If, as has been convincingly argued, the "thinkers and doers" of the eighteenth century formed many of their opinions from the columns of the *Gazette de Leyde*, then the image of Louis XVI as arbiter and mediator of European politics was certainly destroyed by the end of November 1787.[41] The sharp contrast created in the newspaper between exaggerated rhetoric and limited, ineffectual actions made Louis XVI appear as impotent in European politics as he did in the pornographic libels which described his sex life. To the aristocrat Soulavie, Louis XVI was now a "nullity."[42] Foreign observers agreed: "The king," opined the Swedish ambassaor to Versailles, "is nothing."[43]

41. Jeremy D. Popkin, *News and Politics*, ix.

42. Robert Darnton, "Reading, Writing and Publishing in Eighteenth-Century France: A Case Study in the Sociology of Literature," *Daedulus* 100 (1971): 241–56; Jean-Louis Soulavie (l'ainé), *Mémoires Historiques et Politiques du Règne de Louis XVI* (Paris, 1801), 6:175.

43. Albert Sorel quoting Ambassador Baron Eric de Stael-Holstein, *L'Europe et la Révolution Française*, 1:211.

Conclusion: In Retrospect

THE LONG-TERM trends that conditioned the crisis in French diplomacy on the eve of the Revolution would have played out no matter who ruled or made decisions. Britain's rise to power in Europe was only temporarily reversed by the loss of the American colonies. After the war, Britain's growing commerce and navy remained a permanent nightmare to the statesmen at Versailles. At the same time, France's victory in the War of the American Revolution did not provide France with solutions to any of the problems that sapped France's capacity to play the role of great power and arbiter of Europe. Whatever views French ministers or military men had about diplomacy and war, there was always the recurring problem they found difficult to deal with: war overextended the financial system. When France lost control over its finances, it was condemned, sooner or later, either to give up the role of a great power and arbiter or suffer a severe financial and political breakdown.[1]

Institutional flaws are always present in the affairs of government. How humans respond to them, use or counter them, makes a difference. Louis XVI was not a tyrannical or charismatic monarch. But he was sincerely devoted to regenerating France and maintaining France's place as arbiter of Europe. To do this he

1. Lynn Hunt, *Politics, Culture and Class in the French Revolution* (Berkeley, 1984), 6–7.

needed peace to provide France with breathing space for reform and recovery. Thus, he and his two secretaries of state for foreign affairs, Vergennes and Montmorin, performed the difficult labor necessary to establish new policies and new networks of relations. The Franco-Russian Commercial Treaty was part of a plan to arrive at an *entente* with Russia. In the same way, it was hoped that the political implications of the Anglo-French Commercial Treaty would be the beginning of more cooperation between France and Britain, especially in Eastern Europe.

Both initiatives failed. France and Britain were too rigidly locked into a pattern of mistrust, competition, arms race, and war. Whatever trust the negotiations for the Anglo-French Commercial Treaty created, the Dutch crisis destroyed. Perhaps the most tragic diplomatic failure of the last years of the Old Regime was the inability of France and Britain to break through their inherited suspicions and build an understanding based on mutual confidence and interests. The failure was truly a lost opportunity.

By 1789 Louis XVI's reputation as arbiter of Europe had all but vanished. As the mediator in the Russo-Turkish conflict, the French monarch's representative at Constantinople was reduced almost to silence as the czarina's and the sultan's suspicions of France accumulated. In Sweden, the swift intervention of Britain and Prussia to prevent a catastrophic defeat of Gustavus III left the French ambassador in Stockholm startled and, for the most part, ignorant of what was going on. In the Spanish-American dispute over the navigation of the Mississippi, Louis XVI, absorbed with problems closer to home, refused to accept the role of mediator, for fear of embarrassing entanglements with his allies. His refusal to officially declare himself in the debates in the United States over the Constitutional Convention was seen by his own diplomat as a mistake with long-term consequences.

The death of Vergennes in 1787 and the dramatic resignations of Louis XVI's secretaries of the army and navy, the maréchal de Ségur and the maréchal de Castries, as the Dutch crisis developed left Louis XVI without a coherent government and with no one of substantial international experience to advise him. At the same time, the conflicts and disunion within the cabinet encouraged each minister to go his own way. It is, of course, impossible to measure with precision the impact of this situation on Louis XVI's ability to govern. There is no doubt, however, that he now faced the difficult task of carrying on foreign affairs without familiar and capable advisers. The baron de Besenval was convinced that Louis's capacity to make sound decisions was, indeed, severely compromised. Surrounded by so many new faces (there were three controllers-general in three months) and caught between so many conflicting opinions, Besenval believed, Louis XVI did not know what to decide.[2] Nevertheless, XVI was neither inept nor indifferent to the responsibilities of power. He was deeply involved in the discussions and responses to the Dutch crisis, the Swedish episode, the Russo-Turkish war, the financial crisis, and the Assembly of Notables. These concerns consumed an enormous amount of his time. But he also continued to deal conscientiously with other diplomatic affairs, despite the confusing changes of ministers and the bitter conflicts over policies and personalities. Even so, some things were inevitably neglected.

It is tempting to blame Montmorin, the new secretary of state for foreign affairs after the death of the comte de Vergennes in February 1787, for Louis XVI's setbacks in Europe. Montmorin was a seasoned diplomat but with only brief experience as a secretary of state. Very soon he had to deal with an international crisis that would have tested the most experienced and skillful statesman. Montmorin quickly assumed responsibility for the principal diplomatic correspondence with Britain and some of the more important correspondence with the Dutch and other European powers.[3] During the decisive months of August and September of 1787,

2. Baron de Besenval, *Mémoires de M. le Baron de Besenval* (Paris, 1805), 3:275–79.

3. "Montmorin, Armand Marc Cte de," AAE-Personnel, 42:322.

Montmorin's correspondence does, indeed, show signs of inexperi-
ence. For example, in mid-September, he instructed the French
ambassador to the Dutch Republic to notify the Patriots that
France was unable to help them. At the same time, he instructed
Louis XVI's minister in London to warn Britain that Louis had
exhausted all options consistent with his love of peace. France
had no alternative, therefore, but to fulfill its duties to its Dutch
allies.[4] Given his long experience, Vergennes might have found a
less contradictory and less embarrassing way to handle France's
predicament. Perhaps, given his extraordinary diplomatic skills
and his recognition of the importance of public opinion, Vergennes might even have been able to turn the Dutch affair into
some kind of symbolic victory in the eyes of the public. But this is
only speculation.

It is unlikely, however, that Vergennes, had he lived, would have
found a way to eliminate the influence of Britain in the Dutch Republic as long as Britain had the support of the Prussian army.
Above all, he would not have supported his colleagues in the government and those French military officers who claimed that their
and Louis XVI's honor demanded that France rush headlong into
another war so soon after the close of the War of the American
Revolution.[5] Vergennes knew that if France was to be regenerated,
it had to have peace. He had learned from the hard school of experience that wars always cost more than anticipated, last longer
than expected and give one's allies the opportunity to demand the
impossible. And he clearly recognized, as did Louis XVI and
Montmorin, the suicidal nature of rushing into a land war on the
Continent while engaged in a naval war with Britain. It was, Vergennes told Louis XVI in 1784, an "uncontested" truth that France,
as powerful as she was, could not sustain such a "double war." It was

4. Lynn Hunt, *Politics, Culture and Class in the French Revolution* (Berkeley,
1984), 6–7.

5. Baron de Besenval, *Mémoires*, 3:275–79.

of the utmost importance, he argued, that France not precipitously embark on one. He had already learned that this opinion was considered "timid" by his critics. But, he warned, governments too often plunge into wars without having calculated the expenses and the probabilities of long duration. In such cases, he noted, exhaustion of means always dictates a less than honorable peace.

It was, therefore, a capital error, Vergennes concluded, to overextend oneself, to reach beyond one's power and end up with exhaustion and impotence.[6] In short, the relation among war, foreign policy, and finances had to be recognized and respected in all political calculations. Finances, Dupont had reminded Vergennes in 1782, were "the nerves of war."[7] Louis XVI and Montmorin agreed. Montmorin went one step further and completed the equation: "I consider . . . [war], to be the source of all our troubles."[8]

The decision not to intervene in the Dutch Republic was not the act of cowards. Louis XVI and his dovish ministers were not trying to avoid personal danger, because there was no personal danger. Whether France decided to go to war or not, they all would remain at Versailles, "far from danger," safe and secure in the palace.[9] Unlike Louis XIV, for whom war somehow defined his identity as monarch, Louis XVI was not a warrior king. He had never as a child marched through the palace beating a drum in imitation of the Swiss guards.[10] War was not essential to his *gloire*. The question, therefore, boiled down to what values were consulted in the making of foreign policy. Louis XVI decided that France's future did not rest on the outcome of the conflict in the

6. "Observations de M. de Vergennes sur le coup de canon tiré sur l'Escaut 14 November 1784," in L. P. Ségur, *Politique de tous les cabinets*, 3:229–31.

7. Jean-François Labourdette, *Vergennes, ministre principal de Louis XVI* (Paris, 1990), 215–16.

8. Jean-Louis Soulavie (l'aîné), *Mémoires Historiques et Politiques du Règne de Louis XVI* (Paris, 1801) 6:456–72.

9. Restiff de la Bretonne, *La Paysane Pervertie* (Le Hague/Paris, 1784), 189.

10. John B. Wolf, *Louis XIV* (New York, 1968), 23–34, 77–78.

Netherlands. Instead, France's future rested on finding a solution to her financial and political problems. This was the issue that divided Louis's government. Castries, along with Ségur, was articulate and uninhibited in his clamor for plunging France once more into war. He was also the least willing to submit to the scrutiny of others the enormous expenditures and debts of his department of the navy.[11]

Louis XVI's grave diplomatic error during these years grew from a mistaken confidence that Prussia would remain in the French orbit. France and Prussia had for so long cooperated to keep the ambitions of Joseph II in check, it seemed reasonable to assume the cooperation would continue. But Louis XVI and Montmorin seemed not to have understood how thoroughly Frederick William II was personally committed to the support of his sister and to the stadholder in the Dutch Republic. Consequently, at the very moment when Prussia and Britain were concluding a secret accord to guarantee support for the stadholder, Montmorin continued to nourish the hope that France could regain Prussia to her side.[12]

Thus, Louis XVI and his secretaries of state for foreign affairs share responsibility for the retreat of France in foreign affairs. But they were not the only players in the drama. Frederick William II of Prussia apparently welcomed the opportunity to dramatize his assumption to the Prussian throne with an impressive diplomatic and military victory. France's financial troubles, the likelihood that a Russo-Turkish war would remove the danger to his rear, and Britain's aggressive determination to break out of her isolation provided Frederick William II with the perfect opportunity. Gustavus's embarrassment in his war with Russia created an additional occasion to seal the relationship between Prussia, Britain, and the Dutch Republic.

11. Labourdette, *Vergennes*, 212–24.
12. Paul Vaucher, *Receuil des Instructions données aux ambassadeurs et ministres* (Paris, 1965), Angleterre, vol. XXV–2, tome 3, 536.

The crisis in diplomacy and the pre-revolutionary domestic crisis in France influenced each other. The preoccupation with domestic affairs made it extremely difficult for Louis XVI and his ministers to respond promptly to rapidly changing diplomatic situations abroad. Moreover, the financial crisis sharply reduced Louis XVI's range of options in foreign affairs. The divisions bred in the government over diplomatic policy became a part of a pattern of much broader political divisions. The resulting conflicts and frustrations encumbered the government and created openings for new political ideologies and revolutionary solutions. The financial collapse during Colonne's administration further eroded the respect foreign powers ordinarily gave to the French king's authority. As France approached 1789, it was difficult to distinguish the domestic from the diplomatic crisis.

The increasing influence of "public opinion" changed the context of foreign policy as well as domestic politics.[13] Indeed, perhaps the public's distorted *perceptions* of betrayal and neglect represented by the Anglo-French Commercial Treaty of 1786 were more influential in the course of French history than the realities created by the Treaty.[14] France's retreat in the Dutch Republic also damaged the monarchy. To some it was disgraceful, dishonorable, and cowardly. To others it was, at best, necessary but humiliating and unheroic. Whatever the perception, Louis XVI and his ministers stood condemned in the court of public opinion.

The official newspaper, and the foreign and unofficial one, were active forces in the making of French public opinion. Readers of

13. On the development of public opinion as a factor in French politics see: Jack R. Censer and Jeremy D. Popkin, eds., *Press and Politics in Pre-Revolutionary France* (Berkeley, 1987). In what follows I have drawn heavily on the ideas developed by Keith Michael Baker's essay "Politics and Public Opinion under the Old Regime: Some Reflections," 204–46.

14. Marie Donaghay, "The Exchange of Products of the Soil and Industrial Goods in the Anglo-French Commercial Treaty of 1786," *Journal of European History* 19, no. 2 (Fall 1990), 401.

the *Gazette de France* and the *Gazette de Leyde* were important participants in the reform movement that launched France into revolution.[15] The *Gazette de France*, by omissions as well as inclusions, presented to its readers a king apparently indifferent to foreign affairs and preoccupied with the domestic crisis, courtly rituals and family ceremonials. By implication it appeared that Louis XIV did not see foreign affairs as worthy and deserving of his time. On the other hand, the image projected in the *Gazette de Leyde* of Louis XVI and his ministry during the prolonged diplomatic crisis of 1786 and 1787 was quite the opposite. The bombastic statements from Paris and Versailles of what France was going to do if the Dutch were attacked reveal an active and engaged government, but one prone to swollen rhetoric and macho posturing. If the French public who read the *Gazette de Leyde* accepted the notion expressed in the pages of that journal that the king's honor and their honor were one, they could hardly have been satisfied with the performance of their government, especially when that performance was continually compared in the *Gazette de Leyde* with the triumphant performance of England. The *Gazette de Leyde* confirmed Baron de Besenval's opinion that France's diplomacy as well as its finances were in disarray.[16]

By the 1780s it was apparent that public opinion had wrested foreign policy, along with religion and finances, from the secrecy and reserve of the king's cabinet. Thinking and reading French men and women were spectators to the retreat of their monarch in foreign affairs, and they reacted with blame and criticism. The makers of French diplomacy during this period thus labored under the stress of a profound crisis of confidence. And unfortunately for the king's prestige, the monarch, his family, and his court favorites were imperfect vessels whose personal ambitions, greed and

15. Jeremy D. Popkin, "The Gazette de Leyde and French Politics under Louis XVI," in Jack R. Censer and Jeremy D. Popkin, eds., *Press and Politics*, 88.

16. Baron de Besenval, *Mémoires* 3:275.

predilection for feeding from the public purse seemed calculated to further convince an unsympathetic public that they were unworthy to rule.

In retrospect, however, we can be more generous. This was a government plagued by an unusual set of complex problems, some of short, others of long term, and Louis XVI inherited as many of these problems as he created. In this crisis, Louis XVI and his ministers decided for excellent reasons that war was not the solution to their problems. In a very important sense, those responsible for the shaken and distressed government after 1786 were involved in a desperate operation to contain and limit their losses at home as well as in the international arena. Certainly, France lost its position as arbiter of Europe. Louis XVI suffered repeated humiliations, loss of prestige, and influence abroad. And these were, indeed, major defeats. On the other hand, France lost no territory. Louis XVI's sovereignty was never threatened by a foreign power and France did not suffer one more costly war. These afflictions came with the French Revolution. Louis XVI and his secretaries of state for foreign affairs were harried statesmen in a painful but necessary retreat from the devastating results of France's overextended position in Europe, men trying to avoid a suicidal war while working to salvage and rebuild essentials in the tormented years of the pre-revolution. They were overwhelmed, but their performances deserve more recognition than they have ever received. At the very least, their performances should reopen the question of who the heroes really were.

Selected Bibliography

Unpublished Primary Sources

Paris: Archives des Affaires Étrangères

Correspondance Politique: Angleterre; Dannemarck; États-Unis; Hollande; Russie; Suède; Turquie
Mémoires et Documents: France; États-Unis
Documents: Personnel
Finances du Ministère

Nantes: Archives Diplomatiques

Comptabilité

Published Primary Sources

Newspapers

Gazette de France, 1786–90
Gazette de Leyde, 1786–90

Books and Articles

Anonymous [Dupont de Nemours]. *Lettre à la Chambre de Commerce de Normandie*. Rouen and Paris, 1788.
Argenson, Marquis d'. *Considérations sur le Gouvernment Ancien et Present de la France*. Amsterdam, 1765.
Bevan, Charles I., ed. *Treaties and Other International Agreements of the United States of America, 1779–1949*. Washington, D.C., 1971.
Bourne, Henry E., ed. "Correspondance of the Comte de Moustier with the

Comte de Montmorin, 1787–1789." *American Historical Review*, no. 8 (1902–3): 709–33.

Besenval, Baron de. *Mémoires de M. le Baron Besenval.* 2 vols. Paris, 1805.

Boyd, Julian P., ed. *The Papers of Thomas Jefferson.* Vol. 10. Princeton, N.J., 1954.

Chambre de Commerce de Normandy. *Observations de la Chambre de Commerce de Normandie sur le Traité . . . entre la France et l'Angleterre.* Rouen, 1788.

Chance, James F., ed. *British Diplomatic Instructions.* London, 1926, Denmark.

Chastenay, Madame de. *Mémoires* Paris, 1894.

Cook, Chris, and John Stevenson. *British Historical Facts, 1760–1830.* Hamden, Conn., 1980.

Coston, Henri, ed. *Procès de Louis XVI et de Marie Antoinette.* Reprint. Paris, 1981.

DuClos, Charles Pinot. *Mémoires secrètes sur les règnes de Louis XIV et Louis XV.* Paris, 1791.

Favier, Jean-Louis. *Doutes et questions sur le traité de Versilles du 1er mai, 1756.* Paris, 1756.

———. *Conjectures raisonnées sur la situation actuelle de la France dans le système de l'Europe.* Paris, 1793.

Ferrand, Comte de. *Mémoires du Comte de Ferrand, Ministre d'Etat sous Louis XVII.* Paris, 1897.

Fitzpatrick, John C., ed. *The Writings of George Washington.* Vol. 29. Washington, D.C., 1931–44.

Gaillard, Gabriel Henri. *Mélanges académiques, poétiques, littéraires.* Paris, 1806.

Gottschalk, Louis, ed. *The Letters of Lafayette to Washington: 1777–1779.* New York, 1944.

Hurewitz, J. C., ed. *Diplomacy in the Near and Middle East.* Princeton, 1956.

Koch, Christophe G., ed. *Table des traités entre la France et les puissances étrangères . . . suivie d'un recueil des traités et actes diplomatiques.* Vol. 2. Basle, 1802.

Lameth, Alexandre. *Histoire de l'assemblée constituante (1789–1790).* 2 vols. Paris, 1828–29.

Levi, Duc de. *Souvenirs et portraits (1789–1790).* Paris, 1813.

Martens, Fedor F., ed. *Recueil des traités et conventions conclue par la Russie avec les puissances étrangères.* Vol. 91. St. Petersburg, 1874–1909.

Martens, Georg G., ed. *Supplément au recueil des principaux traités.* Vol. 3. Gottingue, 1807.

Minto, Emma Eleanor Elizabeth Elliot, Countess of. *A Memoir of the Right Honorable Hugh Elliot.* Edinburgh, 1868.

Morison, Samuel Eliot. *Sources and Documents Illustrating the American Revolution, 1764–1788, and the Formation of the Federal Constitution.* New York, 1965.

Ozanam, Didier, and Michel Antoine. *Correspondance secrète du Comte de Broglie avec Louis XV (1756–1774)* 2 vols. Paris, 1961.

Parry, Clive. *Consolidated Treaty Series.* Vols. 48–50. Dobbs Ferry, N.Y., 1969.

Raynal, l'abbé. *Histoire philosophiques et politiques des établissements et du commerce des Européannes dans les deux Indes.* Geneva, 1781.

Recueil Des Instructions Aux Ambassadeurs et Ministres de France depuis les Traités de Westphalie jusqu'à la Révolution. Publié sous les auspices de la commission des Archives diplomatiques aux ministère des affaires étrangères. 28 vols. Paris, 1884–1960.

Rousseau, Jean-Jacques. *Political Writings.* Edited by C. E. Vaughan. 2 vols. Cambridge, Mass., 1915.

Saint-Priest, comte de. *Mémoires sur l'Ambassade de France en Turquie.* Paris, 1877.

Ségur, L. P., ed. *Politiques de Tous les Cabinets de L'Europe pendant les Règnes de Louis XV et de Louis XVI.* 3 vols. Paris, 1801.

————. *Mémoires et Souvenirs et Anecdotes.* 2 vols. Paris, 1843.

Soulavie, Jean-Louis (l'ainé). *Mémoires Historiques et Politiques du Règne de Louis XVI.* 6 vols. Paris, 1801.

Tott, Baron de. *Mémoires sur les Turcs et les Tarters.* Amsterdam, 1784.

Vaucher, Paul, ed. *Recueil des instructions aux ambassadeurs et ministres de France . . .* Angleterre. Vol. XXV–2, tome 3.

Wenck, Frederick August W. *Codex juris gentium recentissimi.* Vol. 3. Leipzig, 1781–95.

Secondary Sources: Books

Arnaud-Bouteloup, Jeanne. *Le rôle politique de Marie Antoinette.* Paris, 1929.

Bagis, Ali Ihsan. *The Embassy of Sir Robert Ainsley at Istanbul (1776–1794).* Ph.D. Diss. University of London, 1974.

Bailey, Thomas A. *A Diplomatic History of the American People.* New York, 1950.

Bamford, Paul. *Forest and French Sea Power.* Toronto, 1956.

Bemis, Samuel Flagg. *A Diplomatic History of the United States.* New York, 1936.

————, ed. *The American Secretaries of State and Their Diplomacy*. Vol. 1. New York, 1927.

Black, Jeremy. *British Foreign Policy in an Age of Revolution: 1783–93*. Cambridge, England, 1994.

Blainey, Geoffrey. *The Causes of War*. Melbourne, 1977.

Blanning, T. C. W. *The Origins of the French Revolutionary Wars*. London and New York, 1986.

Bosher, J. F. *French Finances, 1779–1795: From Business to Bureaucracy*. Cambridge, England, 1970.

Braudel, Fernand, and Ernest Labrousse. *Histoire économique et sociale de la France*. Paris, 1970.

Bretonne, Restif de la. *La Paysanne Pervertie*. The Hague and Paris, 1784.

Browning, Oscar. *The Treaty of Commerce between England and France in 1786*. Transactions of the Royal Historical Society. London, 1885.

Castelot, André. *Marie Antoinette*. London, 1957.

Castries, René de la Croix, duc de. *Le Maréchal de Castries: Serviteur de Trois Rois, 1727–1800*. Paris, 1979.

Censer, Jack, and Jeremy Popkin. *Press and Politics in Pre-Revolutionary France*. Berkeley, 1987.

Chambrun, Charles de. *A l'école d'un diplomat:Vergennes* Paris, 1944.

Clamageran, J. J. *Histoire de L'impôt en France*. 3 vols. Paris, 1873.

Cobban, Alfred. *Ambassadors and Secret Agents*. London, 1954.

————. *A History of Modern France*. 2 vols. Baltimore, 1961.

Corvisier, André. *Armies and Societies in Europe, 1574–1789*. Translated by A. T. Siddall. Bloomington, Ind., 1979.

Dakin, Douglas. *Turgot and the Ancien Régime in France*. New York, 1965.

Darling, Arthur Burr. *Our Rising Empire: 1763–1803*. New Haven, 1940.

DeConde, Alexander. *A History of American Foreign Policy*. New York, 1963.

DeWitt, Pierre. *Une Invasion Prussienne en Hollande en 1787*. Paris, 1896.

Doyle, William. *Origins of the French Revolution*. Oxford, 1980.

Dull, Jonathan R. *The French Navy and American Independence*. Princeton, 1975.

Egret, Jean. *The French Prerevolution: 1787–1788*. Translated by Wesley D. Camp. Chicago, 1977.

Eton, William. *A Survey of the Turkish Empire* London, 1809.

Geffroy, A. *Gustave III et la Cour de France*. 2 vols. Paris, 1867.

Gibb, Hamilton, and Harold Bowen. *Islamic Society and the West*. New York, 1950. 2 vols.

Gomel, Charles. *Les Causes Financières de la Révolution Française*. 2 vols. Paris, 1892.

Goodwin, A., ed. *The New Cambridge Modern History*. Vol. 8, *The American and French Revolutions, 1763–93*. Cambridge, England, 1965.

Gottschalk, Louis. *Lafayette between the American and the French Revolution (1783–1789)*. Chicago, 1950.

Hale, William, and Ali Ihsan Bagis, eds. *Four Centuries of Turco-British Relations*. North Yorkshire, 1984.

Hardman, John. *Louis XVI*. New Haven, 1993.

Harris, Robert D. *Necker, Reform Statesman of the Ancien Régime*. Berkeley, 1977.

Hill, Peter P. *French Perceptions of the Early American Republic: 1783–1793*. Philadelphia, 1988.

Hunt, Lynn. *Politiques, Culture and Class in the French Revolution*. Berkeley, 1984.

Israel, Jonathan. *The Dutch Republic: Its Rise, Greatness and Fall, 1477–1806*. Oxford, 1995.

Jarrett, Derek. *The Begetters of Revolution*. Totowa, N.J., 1973.

Jensen, Merrill. *The New Nation: A History of the United States during the Confederation: 1781–1789*. New York, 1962.

Jones, Colin. *The Longman Companion to the French Revolution*. New York, 1988.

Klaits, Joseph. *Printed Propaganda under Louis XIV, Absolute Monarchy and Public Opinion*. Princeton, 1976.

Kaplan, Lawrence. *Colonies into Nation: American Diplomacy, 1763–1801*. New York, 1972.

Kennedy, Paul. *The Rise and Fall of the Great Powers*. New York, 1987.

Labourdette, Jean-François. *Vergennes, ministre principal de Louis XVI*. Paris, 1990.

Lameth, Alexandre. *Histoire de l'assemblée Constituante (1789–1790)*. Paris, 1828.

Lefebvre, Georges. *The Coming of the French Revolution*. Princeton, 1947.

Legohérel, Henri. *Les Trésoriers Généraux de la Marine (1577–1788)*. Paris, 1965.

Leopold, Richard. *The Growth of American Foreign Policy*. New York, 1962.

Levy, Jack S. *War in the Modern Great Power System: 1495–1975*. Lexington, Ky., 1983.

Livet, Georges, and Roland Mousnier. *Histoire général de l'Europe*. Paris, 1980.

Madariaga, Isabel de. *Britain, Russia and the Armed Neutrality of 1780*. New Haven, 1962.

Manceron, Claude. *The French Revolution: Toward the brink, 1785–1787*. New York, 1983.

Marks, Frederick W. *Independence on Trial: Foreign Affairs and the Making of the Constitution*. Baton Rouge, La., 1973.

Matthews, George. *The Royal General Farms in Eighteenth-Century France*. New York, 1958.

McCusker, John J. *Money and Exchange in Europe and America, 1600–1775: A Handbook*. Chapel Hill, N.C., 1978

Merrick, Jeffrey W. *The Desacralization of the French Monarchy in the Eighteenth Century*. Baton Rouge, La., 1990.

Mosser, Françoise.*Intendants des finances au XVIIIe siècle*. Paris, 1978.

Murphy, Orville. *Charles Gravier, Comte de Vergennes; French Diplomacy in the Age of Revolution, 1719–1787*. Albany, N.Y., 1982.

Olivia, L. Jay. *Misalliance: A Study of French Policy in Russia during the Seven Years' War*. New York, 1964.

Oursel, Paul. *La Diplomatie de la France sous Louis XVI*. Paris, 1921.

Ozanam, Denise. *Claude Baudard de Sainte-James: Trésorier Général de la Marine et Brasseur D'affaires: 1738–1787*. Geneva, 1969.

Peyster, Henry de. *Les Troubles de Hollande à la Veille de la Révolution Française, 1780–1795*. Paris, 1905.

Popkin, Jeremy D. *News and Politics in the Age of Revolution: Jean Luzac's 'Gazette de Leyde'*. Ithaca, N.Y., 1989.

———.*Press and Politics in Pre-Revolutionary France*. Berkeley, 1987.

Price, Monroe. *Preserving the Monarchy: The Comte de Vergennes, 1774–1787*. Cambridge, England, 1995.

Rabb, Reginald E. *The Role of William Eden in William Pitt's Liberal Trade Policy*. New York, 1942.

Rain, Pierre. *La Diplomatie française d'Henri IV à Vergennes*. Paris, 1945.

Reilly, Robin. *William Pitt the Younger*. London, 1978.

Riley, James. *The Seven Years War and the Old Regime in France: The Economic and Financial Toll*. Princeton, 1986.

———. *International Government Finance and the Amsterdam Capital Market: 1740–1815*. Cambridge, England, 1980.

Rose, J Holland. *William Pitt and National Revival*. London, 1911.

Roberts, Michael. *Essays in Swedish History*. London, 1967.

Roider, Karl. *Austria's Eastern Question: 1700–1790*. Princeton, 1982.

Samoyault, Jean-Pierre. *Les bureaux du secrétariat d'Etat des affaires étrangères sous Louis XVI*. Paris, 1971.

Schama, Simon. *Citizens: A Chronicle of the French Revolution*. New York, 1989.

———. *Patriots and Liberators: Revolution in the Netherlands, 1788–1813*. New York, 1977.

Sgard, Jean. *Dictionnaire des Journalistes: 1600–1789.* Grenoble, 1979.

Shaw, Stanford. *History of the Ottoman Empire and Modern Turkey.* Cambridge, 1976.

Smith, Adam. *The Wealth of Nations.* New York: Modern Library, 1967.

Solomon, Howard M. *Public Welfare, Science and Propaganda in 17th Century France: The Innovation of Théophraste Renaudot.* Princeton, 1972.

Sorel, Albert. *L'Europe et la Révolution Française.* 6 vols. Paris, 1885.

Stinchcombe, William C. *The American Revolution and the French Alliance.* Syracuse, N.Y., 1969.

Stourm, René. *Les Finances de l'ancien régime et de la Révolution.* 2 vols. Paris, 1885.

Temperley, Harold. *Frederic the Great and Kaiser Joseph.* London, 1915.

Varg, Paul A. *Foreign Policies of the Founding Fathers.* Baltimore, 1970.

Vovelle, Michel. *The Fall of the French Monarchy: 1787–1792.* Translated by Susan Burke. Cambridge, England, 1984.

Wick, Daniel L. *A Conspiracy of Well-Intentioned Men: The Society of Thirty and the French Revolution.* New York, 1987.

Wolf, John B. *Louis XIV.* New York, 1968.

Wright, Quincy. *A Study of War.* Chicago, 1964.

Zeller, Gaston. *Histoire des relations internationales.* 3 vols. Paris, 1955.

Secondary Sources: Articles

Alter, George, and James C. Riley. "How to Bet on Lives: A Guide to Life Contingent Contracts in Early Modern Europe." In *Research in Economic History,* edited by Paul Uselding, 1–53. Greenwich, Conn., 1986.

Anderson, M. S. "Great Britain and the Growth of the Russian Navy in the Eighteenth Century." *Mariner's Mirror* 42 (1953): 132–46.

———. "The Great Powers and the Russian Annexation of the Crimea, 1783–1784." *Slavonic and East European Review* 37 (1958–59): 17–41.

Antoine, Michel. "L'administration centrale des finances en france du XVIe au XVIIIe siècle." *Francia* 9 (1980): 511–33.

Azam, Denise Aimé. "Le Ministère des affaires étrangères et la presse à la fin de l'ancien régime." *Cahiers de la Presse* (July 1938): 428–38.

Bagis, Ali Ihsan. "The Advent of British Interests in the Integrity of the Ottoman Empire." *Hacettepe University Bulletin of Social Sciences,* no. 1 (December 1978): 102–18.

Bergès, Louis. "Le Roi ou la nation? Un Débat de conscience après Varennes entre diplomates français (juillet, 1791)." *Revue d'histoire diplomatique,* no. 1–2 (1984): 31–46.

Birn, Raymond. "Livre et Société after Ten Years: Formation of a Discipline." *Studies on Voltaire and the Eighteenth Century* 151 (1976): 287–312.

Black, Jeremy. "The Marquis of Carmathen and Relations with France, 1784–1787." *Francia* 12 (1985): 283–303.

———. "Sir Robert Ainsley: His Majesty's Agent Provacateur? British Foreign Policy and the International Crisis of 1787." *European History Quarterly* 14 (1984): 253–83.

Bosher, J. F. "Current Writings on Administration and Finance in 18th-Century France." *Journal of Modern History* 53 (March 1981): 73–83.

———. "The French Government's Motives in the Affaire Du Canada, 1761–1763." *English Historical Review* 96 (January 1981): 59–78.

———. "The Premiers Commis Des Finances in the Reign of Louis XVI." *French Historical Studies* 3, no. 4 (1964): 475–94.

Bossenga, G. "From Corps to Citizenship: The Bureaux des finances before the French Revolution." *Journal of Modern History* 58 (1986): 610–42

Bruguière, Michel. "Louis XVI's Receivers-general and Their Successors." *French History* 1, no. 2 (1987): 238–56.

Burley, Peter. "A Bankrupt Régime." *History Today* 34 (January 1984): 36–42.

Cahen, Léon. "Une nouvelle interpretation du traité Franco-Anglais de 1786–1787." *Revue historique* 185 (1939): 257–85.

Cavanaugh, G. J. "Nobles, Privileges and Taxes in France: A Revision Reviewed." *French Historical Studies* 8 (Fall 1974): 681–92.

Charles-Roux, François. "La politique française en Egupt à la fin du XVIIIe siècle." *Revue historique* 92 (1906): 531–53.

Crout, Robert Rhodes. "In Search of a Just and Lasting Peace: The Treaty of 1783, Louis XVI, Vergennes and the Regeneration of the Realm." *The International Review* 5 (August 1983): 363–98.

Darnton, Robert. "Reading, Writing and Publishing in Eighteenth-Century France: A Case Study in the Sociology of Literature." *Daedalus* 100 (1971): 241–56.

Donaghay, Marie. "The Best Laid Plans: French Executions of the Anglo-French Commercial Treaty of 1786." *European History Quarterly* 14 (1984): 401–22.

———. "Calonne and the Anglo-French Commercial Treaty of 1786." *Journal of Modern History* 50, no. 3 (1978): ii [abstract]. For entire article see: Supplement, 1157–84. University Microfilms.

———. "The Exchange of Products of the Soil and Industrial Goods in the Anglo-French Commercial Treaty of 1786." *Journal of European Economic History* 19 (Fall 1990): 377–401.

————. "The Ghosts of Ruined Ships: The Commercial Treaty of 1786 and the Lessons of the Past." In *Proceedings of the 1981 Consortium on Revolutionary Europe* (Athens, Ga. 1981): 111–18.

————. "The Maréchal de Castries and the Anglo-French Commercial Negotiations of 1786–1787." *Historical Journal* 22, no. 2 (1979): 285–312.

————. "Textiles and the Anglo-French Commercial Treaty of 1786." *Textile History* 13, no. 2 (1982): 205–24.

————. "Trust Misplaced: Anglo-French Relations after Vergennes." Unpublished paper delivered at the annual meeting of the Southern Historical Association, Orlando, Fla. November 1993.

————. "Vergennes and the Anglo-French Commercial Treaty of 1786." Unpublished paper delivered at the annual meeting of the Society for French Historical Studies, Columbia, S.C. Spring 1988.

————. "The Vicious Circle: The Anglo-French Commercial Treaty of 1786 and the Dutch Crisis of 1787." Unpublished paper delivered at the annual meeting of the Consortium on Revolutionary Europe. Tallahassee, Fla. Fall 1989.

Doyle, William O. "The Parlements of France and the Breakdown of the Old Régime, 1774–1788." *French Historical Studies* 6, no. 4 (1970): 415–58.

Duniway, Clyde Augustus. "French Influence on the Adoption of the Federal Constitution." *American Historical Review* 9 (October 1903 to July 1904): 304–9.

Fox, Frank. "Negotiating with the Russians: Ambassador Ségur's Mission to Saint Petersburg, 1784–1789." *French Historical Studies* 7, no. 1 (1971), 47–71.

Frey, Linda and Marsha. "Fatal Diplomacy, 1541." *History Today* 40 (August 1990): 10–16.

————. "The Reign of the Charlatan Is Over: The French Revolutionary Attack on Diplomatic Practice." *Journal of Modern History* 65, no. 4 (December 1993) 706–45.

Gilbert, Felix. "The 'New' Diplomacy of the Eighteenth Century." *World Politics* 5, no. 1 (October 1951): 1–38.

Glete, Jan. "Sails and Oars, Warships and Navies in the Baltic during the 18th Century (1700–1815)." In *Les Marines de Guerre Européenes, XVII–XVIIIe siècles*, edited by José Merino and Jean Mayer. Paris, 1985.

Goff, T. J. A., and Jean Meyer. "Les Constructions navales en France pendant la seconde moitié du XVIIIe siècle." *Annales, Economies, Sociétés, Civilizations* 26 (January-February 1971): 173–85.

Goodwin, A. "Calonne, the Assembly of Notables of 1787 and the Origins of the Révolte Nobiliaire." *English Historical Review* 61 (1946): Part I, 202–34; Part II, 329–77.

Guéry, Alain. "Les Finances de la monarchie Français sous l'ancien régime." *Annales, Economies, Sociétés, Civilizations* 33 (mars-avril 1978): 216–39.

Harris, Robert D. "Necker's Compte rendu of 1781: A Reconsideration." *Journal of Modern History* 42, no. 2 (June 1970): 180.

Labourdette, Jean-François. "Vergennes ou la tentation du `ministeriat.'" *Revue historique* 275, no. 1 (1986): 73–107.

Lynn, John. "Recalculating French Army Growth during the *Grand Siècle*, 1610–1715." *French Historical Studies* 18, no. 4 (Fall 1994): 881–906.

Mathias, Peter, and Patrick O'Brien. "Taxation in Britain and France, 1715–1810. A Comparison of the Social and Economic Incidence of Taxes Collected by the Central Government." *European Economic History Review* 33 (1980): 601–850.

Moreux, René. "La situation de la France dans le Levant à la fin du XVIIIe siècle." *Revue d'histoire moderne et contemporaine* 3 (1901–3): 137–55.

Morineau, Michel. "Budgets de l'état et gestion des finances royales en France au dix-huitième siècle.'" *Revue historique* 264 (October-December 1980): 289–336.

Moustier, Renaud, comte de. "Les Etats-Unis au lendemain de la guerre de l'indépendance." *Revue d'histoire diplomatique* 6 (1892): 518–40.

Parker, Geoffrey. "The Military Revolution, 1560–1660–A Myth?" *Journal of Modern History* 48 (June 1976): 195–214.

Popkin, Jeremy. "The French Revolutionary Press: New Findings and New Perspectives." *Eighteenth-Century Life* 5 (Summer 1979): 90–104.

Poussou, Jean-Pierre. "Le dynamisme de l'économie française sous Louis XVI." *Revue economique* 40, no. 6 (1989): 965–84.

Ragsdale, Hugh. "Montmorin and Catherine's Greek Project: Revolution in French Foreign Policy." *Cahiers du monde Russe et Sovietique* 27 (1986): 27–44.

Regemorter, J. L. van. "Commerce et politique: preparation et négotiation du traité franco-russe de 1787," *Cahiers du monde Russe et Sovietique* 4, no. 3 (July-September 1963): 230–57.

Riley, James C. "Dutch Investments in France, 1781–1787." *Journal of Modern History* 33 (December 1973): 732–60.

———. "French Finances, 1727–1768." *Journal of Modern History* 59 (June 1987): 209–43.

———, and John J. McCuster. "Money Supply, Economic Growth and the Quantity Theory of Money: France, 1650–1788." *Explorations in Economic History* 20 (1983): 274–93.

Schaeper, Thomas J. "French and English Trade after the Treaty of Utrecht: The Missions of Anisson and Fénellon in London, 1713–1714." *British Journal for Eighteenth-Century Studies* 9 (1986): 1–18.

Schmidt, Charles. "La crise industrielle de 1788 en France." *Revue historique* 97 (January-April, 1908): 78–94.

Sée, Henri. "The Normandy Chamber of Commerce and the Commercial Treaty of 1786." *Economic History Review* 2 (1929–1930): 308–13.

Sturgill, Claude C. "Observations of the French War Budget, 1781–1790." *Military Affairs* 48 (October 1984): 180–87.

Taillemite, Etienne. "La Marine et ses chefs pendant la guerre de l'indépendance Américaine." *Revue historique des armées*, no. 4 (1983): 20–31.

Taylor, George. "The Paris Bourse on the Eve of the French Revolution, 1781–1789." *American Historical Review* 67 (1962): 951–77.

———. Review of J. F. Bosher's *French Finances, 1779–1795*. *Journal of Economic History* 31 (1971): 949–53.

Vroil, Jules de. "Le traité de commerce de 1786." *Journal des economistes*. 3ᵉ série, 17 (1870): 56–65.

Young, David. "Montesquieu's View of Despotism and His Use of Travel Literature." *Review of Politics* 40 (1978): 392–405.

Index

The Diplomatic Retreat of France and Public Opinion on the Eve of the French Revolution, 1783–1789 was composed in Adobe Caslon by The Marathon Group, Durham, North Carolina; printed on 60-pound Natural Smooth and bound by Braun-Brumfield, Inc., Ann Arbor, Michigan; and designed and produced by Kachergis Book Design, Pittsboro, North Carolina.

DATE DUE

UPI   PRINTED IN U.S.A.